WITHDRAWN
NDSU

Ouspensky

By the same author
NO EASY IMMORTALITY
GURDJIEFF IN ACTION

OUSPENSKY,

The Unsung Genius.

J. H. REYNER

(John Hereward)

London
GEORGE ALLEN & UNWIN
Boston   Sydney

© J. H. Reyner, 1981
This book is copyright under the Berne Convention. No reproduction without permission. All rights reserved.

**George Allen & Unwin (Publishers) Ltd,
40 Museum Street, London WC1A 1LU, UK**

George Allen & Unwin (Publishers) Ltd,
Park Lane, Hemel Hempstead, Herts HP2 4TE, UK

Allen & Unwin Inc.,
9 Winchester Terrace, Winchester, Mass 01890, USA

George Allen & Unwin Australia Pty Ltd,
8 Napier Street, North Sydney, NSW 2060, Australia

First published in 1981

British Library Cataloguing in Publication Data

Reyner, J. H.
  Ouspensky.
  1. Ouspensky, P. D.   2. Philosophers – Soviet
  Union – Biography
  I. Title
  197'.21   B4249.0/

ISBN 0-04-294122-9

Set in 11 on 13 point Baskerville by Grove Graphics, Tring
and printed in Great Britain
by A. Wheaton & Co, Exeter

B
4279
U74
R48
1981

Contents

1	Who was Ouspensky?	page	1
2	Literary Ventures		7
3	Peter and Damien		14
4	St. Petersburg		19
5	Interlude		27
6	Meeting with Gurdjieff		36
7	The Caucasus		43
8	London		49
9	The Prieuré		54
10	The Break with Gurdjieff		61
11	London Again		70
12	Madame Ouspensky		76
13	Maurice Nicoll		83
14	Lyne Place		89
15	America		96
16	Last Days in England		103
17	Ouspensky Fourth Dimension		108
	Relevant Reading		114
	Major Books by P. D. Ouspensky		115

Foreword

The name of P. D. Ouspensky is well known in psychological circles as the foremost exponent of the ideas brought from the East by the Caucasian mystic, G. I. Gurdjieff. He has indeed been called the Plato to Gurdjieff's Socrates.

This very dedication, however, tends to obscure his individual genius. He was an original thinker of unusual calibre and had achieved recognition not only in his native Russia but also in Europe and America before he ever met Gurdjieff and the teaching to which he devoted the rest of his life.

He is usually regarded as an austere intellectual but the real Ouspensky was a warm and compassionate man who verified for himself the ideas about which he spoke. As a result, his writings have a quality of personal experience for which posterity has every reason to be profoundly grateful.

This is the genius I have attempted to portray, not as a detailed biography but more as a portrait of a very human character. The narrative necessarily includes occasional personal comment based on forty years experience of the Gurdjieff philosophy as a student and, more recently, as a teacher.

My thanks are due to his publishers for permission to reproduce certain extracts, and also to the many friends and colleagues who have helped me in the preparation of this work, and particularly to John Waterhouse for his delightful sketch of the essential Ouspensky which appears on the jacket.

October 1980　　　　　　　　　　　　　　　　J. H. REYNER

I

Who was Ouspensky?

In the early nineteen-twenties word began to spread in London of a Russian philosopher, P. D. Ouspensky, who had given some lectures to the Quest Society on the nature of the real world which lies behind the appearances of the senses. The ideas aroused considerable attention and he continued to develop them in a succession of private meetings at a house in Warwick Gardens, Kensington.

His audiences were particularly attracted by the eminently practical nature of his expositions. He was a mathematician of considerable calibre who had published a number of books about possible worlds of higher dimensions, and the altogether different qualities of consciousness necessary to comprehend them. He felt, however, that the existence of such realms was not just a matter of conjecture and that there must be places where practical contact with these higher levels had always existed through the ages. He had therefore travelled extensively both in Europe and the East in search of centres where ancient wisdom had been preserved.

He was only partially successful until, almost by accident, he met a Caucasian mystic named Gurdjieff who had been similarly seeking the truth and had returned from a Sufi monastery in the Hindu Kush with some remarkable ideas. These Ouspensky immediately recognised as providing the consummation of his own thinking, and he devoted the rest of his life to the interpretation of these vividly new concepts.

Ouspensky: The Unsung Genius

The basis of this new philosophy was that the troubles of the world stem from man's illusion that he is fully conscious and in complete command of himself. Actually, all his ordinary behaviour, his actions, his feelings, and even his thoughts are the result of entirely mechanical responses to the random events of life. But he has the ability to become aware of himself and begin to perform his various duties consciously, which changes the whole quality of his experience and enables him to make a significant use of the events of the day instead of being entirely at their mercy; and as an important corollary, a man acting consciously serves something higher than himself.

These ideas were refreshing to the bewildered world emerging from the catastrophe of the First World War and they received considerable support from influential people. They were to form the basis of a new system of thought which has since spread throughout the whole of the Western world. It was no new religion but a reappraisal of the old, involving the awakening of the mind. This is the 'repentance' constantly urged by Christ nearly two thousand years ago, an injunction not understood today because the meaning of the word has become degraded to imply regret for one's misdeeds. In the original Greek the word is *metanoia* which means expansion of the mind, which is a very different concept. The significant impact of Ouspensky's lectures arose from his ability to interpret these ideas in the scientific language of the modern era.

What manner of man was this Russian scholar who spoke English with some difficulty and yet was able to inspire his audience so profoundly? Today many people know him only through his books which, together with the occasional photograph on their jackets, create the impression of an austere and remote individual, a master of the lucid phrase living in the rarefied atmosphere of the intellectual world.

This is a quite misleading impression. Actually he was a very generous individual with his due quota of human frailties. In his personal contacts he displayed a warmth of understanding

Who was Ouspensky?

and a refreshing sense of humour, though he had a ruthless contempt for trivialities. But he was a Russian, with all the strengths and weaknesses of that race, so that in his public appearances, whether as lecturer or teacher, his manner could not be other than authoritarian, and this is reflected in the outstanding quality of his writings.

Today this is all we have, since he died in 1947. Yet to regard this legacy as no more than an exercise of intellectual erudition is to forgo completely the inspiration behind his interpretations. To share his visions we must try to understand the real nature of this gentle genius.

* * *

Pyotr Demianovich Uspenskii, to give him his Russian style (which incidentally shows how his name should be spoken), was born in Moscow in 1878. His father was an officer in the Survey Department of the Government, very fond of music and painting, and a good mathematician interested particularly in the concept of the fourth dimension, which was a popular topic of the day. His mother was a painter and was well versed in Russian and French literature, while there appears to have been a particularly happy relationship with his grandparents. His grandfather was an artist specialising in church paintings, which was a highly honourable profession at that time, while he speaks with affection of the stories of old Moscow life with which he and his sister were regaled by his grandmother.

This cultural background naturally influenced his early years. He began to read at the age of three and used to say that he had clear recollections of events of that period such as the Moscow Exhibition of 1882 and the coronation of Alexander III in 1883. He recalls in particular the enormous impressions he received at the age of six from reading two of the classics of Russian literature, Lermontoff's *Hero of Our Time* and Turgenev's *A Sports-*

man's Sketches, both of which were sharply critical of the unimaginative acceptance of the established order (and earned their authors periods of imprisonment).

He became increasingly interested in what he felt were the realities of life. Poetry and painting excited him and at about eight years of age he began to take a keen delight in natural science; everything about plants and animals aroused the sense of wonder which was to remain with him all his life.

School work he found dull, no doubt because of his deepening mistrust of mechanical routine. He determined to eschew academic distinction and made no attempt to take any degrees. Fortunately the boys at the school were left very much to themselves and he began to study psychology and the philosophy of Nietzsche which he discovered when he was sixteen.

At eighteen he left school and began to earn a living as a journalist and translator. It was an interesting life, but not wholly to be believed in. He recalled a picture-book which he had as a child with the intriguing title *Obvious Absurdities*. Some of the examples were clear enough, such as a carriage with square wheels, but others seemed at first to be quite normal and it was not until later that he saw that most of the established customs of life are equally absurd. He began to develop the insatiable urge to question everything, to challenge all the things we usually take for granted, and this was to characterise his whole life.

He was even more dissatisfied with science where he saw the same dead hand of orthodoxy. He said at the time that the professors were killing science in the same way as priests were destroying religion. He was particularly disappointed with the conventional interpretations of the fourth dimension. This was a subject which appealed strongly to his scientific mind, no doubt inspired by his father's interest in the idea, but it had become something of a popular cult.

Interest had been aroused in scientific circles by C. W. Hinton's classic book *A New Era of Thought*. This postulated that while we are familiar with the three dimensions of space – length, breadth and height – there is a fourth dimension along which the events of life travel in succession, creating the illusion of passing time. Hinton maintained that we were virtually unaware of this and by way of illustration he imagined a country called Flatland populated by a race of two-dimensional beings who could only recognise length and breadth, but had no conception of height. He showed how such a race would be completely happy in their world, in which they would accept as quite natural various limitations, such as never being able to see the back of people. They would be subject to many supernatural manifestations as, for example, the impact of some object from a higher level which might annihilate scores of individuals by an 'act of God'.

It is easy to see how the familiar three-dimensional world will be subject to similar limitations, and hence to envisage the possibilities of a four-dimensional realm. Any such speculation, however, is usually entirely subjective, assuming that the four-dimensional world is some kind of extension of the known conditions. Ouspensky regarded this as completely wrong. A world of higher dimensions would, he felt, be subject to entirely different and superior laws and that a proper perspective could only be attained by realising that the objects and events of ordinary life were merely interpretations by the senses of a much more comprehensive but invisible world in which lay the causes of all earthly manifestations. This he expressed in a book entitled *The Fourth Dimension,* published in Moscow in 1898, when he was only twenty, and which earned for him immediate respect from the mathematical fraternity of the time.

He wrote several other books on occult subjects, which were published in Russia, but are of minor significance because their subject matter was incorporated in his two major works, *Tertium Organum* and *A New Model of the Universe* which were to appear several years later. Nevertheless one can see in these early writings the emergence of that genius for lucid exposition which was to characterise his subsequent activities. He was intuitively aware of the distinction between the visible and invisible worlds, but whereas the existence of the real or spiritual world had hitherto been a matter of religious faith he was concerned to demonstrate its actual existence, hidden from the normal gaze by the limitations of conventional logic, but accessible to the higher levels of consciousness which man can develop if he chooses.

It was, in fact, this intuitive belief which was the motivation of his early years, when everything was new and exciting.

2

Literary Ventures

The turn of the century found Ouspensky occupied in a variety of literary pursuits. He had left school at the age of eighteen, and having acquired a useful knowledge of foreign languages he was able to obtain employment as a journalist and translator. He wrote for several journals but principally as foreign correspondent on one of the Moscow newspapers. He confesses to having been anarchistically inclined, but in the broadest sense, being at odds with all forms of mechanical behaviour, whether radical or conservative, and was no party to the secret revolutionary societies with which the intelligentsia of the time sympathised.

In this activity he was fortunate since it was in keeping with his innate love of writing, which was part of the spirit of inquiry inherent in his Essence. This is a term used by Gurdjieff to describe the real part of a man as distinct from the superficial characteristics which have to be acquired from the experiences of life, which he called Personality. If the circumstances of a person's life are in accord with his Essential tendencies the possibilities for development are evidently increased, but this is relatively rare, for there are many people whose daily activities are by no means in harmony with their secret aspirations.

Actually this concept of Essence was one of the most inspiring ideas which he was later to learn from Gurdjieff, who taught that man was a dual entity, part real, part artificial. The real part, which he called Essence, is spiritual in character and belongs to a much higher level of the Universe than the physical body which is only a temporary habitation. In order to adapt itself to the conditions of everyday life the body has to build up a vast network of associations which form what is called the Personality, and it is this which determines the reactions to events. But this Personality is an artefact, acquired by education and experience, much of it implanted by parents, teachers and in general by people other than oneself; so that while Essence is one's own, Personality is not.

Essence, however, is undeveloped and the purpose of the sojourn on earth is the search for suitable nourishment so that it can grow in stature. This can be provided by a *conscious* use of the acquired faculties so that Essence feeds on Personality rather like the germ of an egg feeds on its surrounding material until it has grown sufficiently to break out of its shell. But this technique of making a conscious use of the events of life is something which has to be learned, and it starts with the realisation that in the ordinary way one's behaviour is not conscious. If a man believes only in his Personality no growth of Essence is possible.

However, these were ideas of which the young Ouspensky was not yet aware. It is clear that he found life both congenial and exciting. His journalistic work was not very demanding and he took the opportunity to broaden his education by travel in Russia and Europe and by reading occult literature of various kinds to reinforce his search for a bridge between the visible and invisible worlds. During this period he came across the idea of recurrence which was to fascinate him for the rest of his life. This is a very ancient concept found in the Indian Vedas and expounded extensively by Pythagoras in the sixth century BC which says that everything repeats in its own aeon. Time is not an ever-rolling stream flowing into some undefined infinity, but pursues a circular path so that in due course it comes back to the starting point and the past is repeated.

Ouspensky realised that this was an idea very much in accord

Literary Ventures

with his thinking about the fourth dimension, which he had always regarded as merely one of the parameters in a realm of a higher order, a realm in which lay the patterns of the events of life which are brought into being by the transit of time. If so, the familiar progression from past to future should be seen as an illusion, an interpretation by the senses of a transit through the real world. Given this premise there is no reason why this transit should not be capable of being repeated, perhaps many times if the level of consciousness remains unchanged.

It is an idea which requires thinking beyond conventional attitudes and Ouspensky elaborated it in some detail as part of the philosophy which he was developing at the time. Meanwhile, as a relaxation, he wrote a novel about a character called Ivan Osokin who, in reviewing his life, realises the many mistakes and wrong choices which he has made. If only, he feels, that he could make a fresh start he would be able to avoid these stupidities and make much more effective use of his opportunities. His thoughts are overheard by a divine power and he is actually given the chance to live his life again; but in the event he repeats the life exactly, meeting the same events in the same way and nothing is changed. Ouspensky draws the parallel of a cinema film in which the life is already recorded and is brought into play in passing time by being run through the projector.

The draft, in fact, was originally written in 1905 as a film script, but was not released until 1915 when Ouspensky re-wrote it as a novel, entitled *Kinemadrama*, which was published in St. Petersburg in that year. It was later translated into English and published in 1947, shortly before his death, under the title *The Strange Life of Ivan Osokin*.

Superficially, the theory of recurrence would appear to preclude the possibility of free will and to reinforce the grim doctrines of predestination still held in some quarters. Ouspensky's insight perceived that such interpretations are illusions of sense-based thinking. Actually, if properly understood it is a concept of great mercy because it contains the implicit possibility of change. The path through the real world is not rigidly confined. The recurrence of the life is only repeated exactly so long as the successive events are interpreted entirely mechanically in the same stereotyped way. If there is some awareness the reactions may be more conscious in which case the path may be modified; but this would involve consciousness of a different order.

The concept of different orders or levels of consciousness is a fundamental tenet of the Gurdjieff-Ouspensky philosophy. According to this idea the Universe is a structure of much greater magnitude than the physical world observed by the senses, being in fact a structure of successively more detailed interpretations of the will of the Supreme or Absolute Creator. Each of these stages is a discrete entity having its own characteristics and laws, only the lowest being capable of being observed by the physical senses.

Each stage or level has its own intelligence and consciousness concerned with the maintenance of its allotted functions, part of which are concerned with the control and direction of the level immediately lower in the scale. Thus the familiar (phenomenal) world obeys clearly defined laws laid down by cosmic intelligence.

The behaviour of man in his normal condition is entirely controlled by the laws of the phenomenal world, but he is created with the ability to respond to the direction of higher levels of intelligence. If he succeeds in doing this he can make different and more significant use of the experiences of life. Esoteric teaching, in fact, says that the real object of the sojourn on earth is the recognition of and submission to these higher levels of intelligence.

* * *

Ideas are like seeds. They do not, and cannot display their full glory initially. They have first to find suitable ground in which to take root. Then if they receive adequate care and nourishment they may burgeon and bear fruit. Ouspensky's genius lay in what could be called his active patience – a quality very different from a Micawber-like waiting for something to turn up. He intuitively recognised the potentiality of ideas which came into his mind, but knew that they required to be nurtured. He would put them aside to be worked on, to be continually reformulated as his understanding developed, not expecting any complete solution in logical terms. Yet by that very work the ideas would come alive and could be communicated to others.

Hence at this time he wrote several books, some of which were published later, while others remained mere exercises. His main preoccupation, however, was the preparation of an ambitious treatise which was to be the key to the enigmas of the world (and was actually so described in the sub-title when it was ultimately published). Its theme was that we live in a conscious Universe, to understand which it is necessary to develop higher qualities of self-consciousness than are employed for the activities of everyday life. By the very magnitude of its scope it was a task which occupied many years, particularly in view of the meticulous attention to detail which characterised all his writing, and it was not until 1912 that it appeared under the title *Tertium Organum*.

Its progress was not uninterrupted. Conditions in Russia were becoming turbulent. There were strikes and disorders which culminated in the armed insurrection of 1905, and although this was suppressed the discontent remained. Nor was the unrest confined to Russia. The world in general was muttering. His writing lost momentum and was in need of some additional impetus. Later, when he met Gurdjieff, he was to discover the law of octaves, in which there are places where the progress may be temporarily impeded so that some shock is necessary if the octave is to proceed. At the time he simply knew intuitively that some change of direction was required.

He refers to this feeling of having come to a dead end in a book which he published some years later entitled *A New*

Model of the Universe. In the foreword he records his reactions one morning in the editorial office of the Moscow daily paper *The Morning* for which he was working at the time. He has just received the foreign papers and has to write an article on the forthcoming Hague Conference of 1907. What, he wonders, is it all in aid of? To quote his words:

> French, German, English, Italian papers. Phrases, phrases, sympathetic, critical, ironical, blatant, pompous, lying and, worst of all, utterly automatic, phrases which have been used a thousand times, and will be again on entirely different, perhaps contradictory occasions. I have to make a survey of all these words and opinions, pretending to take them seriously and then, just as seriously, to write something on my own account. But what can I say? It is all so tedious. Diplomats and all kinds of statesmen will gather together and talk, papers will approve or disapprove, sympathise or not sympathise. Then everything will be as it was, or even worse.
>
> P. D. Ouspensky, *A New Model of the Universe*

Words written nearly seventy-five years ago, but having an uncomfortable ring of truth today. He decides that the article will not be written that day – perhaps not at all. Humanity will lose nothing if there is one article the less on the Hague Conference. A great many 'wicked' thoughts occur to him on these matters of such spurious importance – none of them printable.

He opens the drawer of his desk and is confronted with some of the books he is reading at the moment – *The Occult World, Life After Death, Atlantis and Lemuria*, and many others. They may seem perhaps impractical and even naive, yet they have a strange flavour of truth, the promise of vistas beyond the arid deserts of materialism.

He decides to set aside his writing for a time, to abandon his ordinary activities and seek some of the ancient cultures.

Literary Venture

So he embarks on a series of travels through Asia Minor, Greece and Egypt, where perhaps he will discover some more real values; which in fact he did, and returned to Russia two years later to resume his writing with renewed impetus.

3

Peter and Damien

At this point one has the impression of an earnest and dedicated young man of thirty who has a clear idea of what he wants to do and has already set his foot on the path. It is indeed his journey over this route in which we are particularly interested, but this intellectual quest is only one aspect of his character. He was an entirely normal man with all the hopes and aspirations of youth and a well-developed emotional and artistic faculty, though this later became overshadowed by his preoccupation with the search for truth.

It was a tradition in the Ouspensky family that the names of Peter and Damien were passed on alternately from father to son and these two names typify distinctly different characteristics. The Damiens were world-rejecting aesthetics while the Peters were concerned with the good things of life both physical and artistic, and the Ouspensky with whom we are concerned was influenced by both these ancestral traits. From the age of about twelve he became extremely interested in art and developed some ability for sketching, as indeed was only to be expected from the influence of his parents. He began to be interested in old Russian prints which he started to collect and in fact took a number of them with him when he went to England, as Stanley Nott remarks in his account of his meeting with the Ouspenskys at Gadsden in Kent. One particularly interesting feature of his early youth is the frequent strong feeling of *déja vu*, the strange familiarity with a situation as if one had experienced it before. Both he and his younger sister, of whom he was very fond, had this kind of experience, and sometimes played a game of sitting at their window and predicting what was going to happen in the streets outside. They did not discuss this with their parents because, as his sister said, 'They don't understand anything anyway.' There is no doubt that this kind of practical experience was responsible for his later interest in the idea of recurrence.

His artistic appreciation was enhanced by a visit to Paris with his mother in 1898 and although when he returned to Russia he took up journalism and began to make more use of his intellectual faculties he was by no means a solitary figure but enjoyed convivial company and good food and wine in the exercise of his 'Peter' characteristics. He is described as being warm and generous, open-hearted and excellent company and it seems that it was not until he began to embark on his serious pursuits that he subordinated these aspects of his character to the more intellectual approach.

After his return from Paris in 1898 he seems to have been considerably upset by the death of his mother shortly afterwards and he set out on a series of travels to the more remote parts of Russia, presumably in an attempt to gain more human experience, and many years later he would reminisce about his adventures to Dr. and Mrs. Nicoll. He described in particular the trick of repaying the very generous hospitality which he found in these peasant tribes. The technique was to express admiration for some very small and inexpensive article which by tradition the host would then press him to accept. It was then possible for Ouspensky to make a return gift of something valuable for which purpose he used to carry round with him a small stock of revolvers.

In general, however, there is little record of his activities during the first few years of the century though one can obtain certain indications from his book *The Strange Life of Ivan*

Osokin which he completed in 1905. It seems that this book was to a large extent autobiographical. The hero went through the same kind of experiences as Ouspensky himself. He was at odds with conventional attitudes and was expelled from school for a childish prank. Ouspensky himself was always at odds with his tutors though, as far as is known, was not actually expelled. The young Osokin has a passionate love affair which is abruptly terminated and Ouspensky later admitted that the heroine in the novel was based on an actual person and one surmises that he, himself, had had a similarly dramatic and unfortunate experience.

All this is interesting as showing that the young Ouspensky was no paragon. He went through the usual adolescent experiences with the accompanying pleasures and pains, which helped him when he came to write on the subject of love in *Tertium Organum* a little later on. It was indeed one of Ouspensky's principal assets that he made the effort to obtain practical experience of subjects about which he subsequently wrote. This was exemplified by his treatment of the subject of dreams about which he was beginning to interest himself at that time. He believed that dreams were the result of some kind of subconscious mental activity of which one normally remembers very little on awakening. He decided, therefore, to try to develop techniques by which dreams could be observed objectively. One method was to try to alert the mind on the point of going to sleep so that it could be ready to observe any dream sequence which followed. An alternative method was to prepare the mind to record a dream immediately on awakening. He told himself that if he could become aware of the fact that he was asleep he might find the possibility of continuing the dreams and perhaps discovering what lay behind them. He came to the conclusion that what he called simple dreams were the result of unconscious associations but that there were more significant dreams arising from unsuspected associations of a superior quality and these could very well communicate information from higher levels in the Universe. He suggested indeed that this kind of information could be available during the normal so-called waking state but that because of the preoccupation with the ordinary affairs of life we were unable to hear it. This was an idea which was greatly reinforced when he subsequently met Gurdjieff.

In 1905 he was very distressed by the fact that his beloved younger sister had been imprisoned for her association with a group having subversive tendencies, and he was even more disturbed when she died in prison a few years later. This, following on the heels of his unhappy love affair left him very despondent and his enthusiasm was at a low ebb. However, about this time he came into contact with a young widow, Sophie Grigorevna, with whom a curious relationship developed which appears to have lifted him out of his depression. She was a few years older than him, having been born in 1874, and had already been married twice, the first time to a fellow student at the age of 16. Her second husband was a mining engineer with whom she travelled to remote parts of Russia, and by whom she had two children. The first, a boy, was killed in an accident early in life but the daughter grew up and in due course (1919) provided them with a grandson, Lonia.

It was one of those strange conjunctions of opposites which often seems to inspire genius, for they were of quite different disposition. She was a woman of the world, extrovert and selfish, in marked contrast to Ouspensky's introvert and generous nature. They each maintained their separate establishments with no thought of a closer relationship. However, with the imminence of revolution in 1917 it seemed prudent to legalise their association and they went through a form of marriage. She remained with him for the rest of his life, sharing the hardships and vicissitudes of the turbulent years which were to follow.

When in 1915 Ouspensky met Gurdjieff he took her with him on several occasions. She responded immediately to the ideas, as well as to the man himself, for whom she developed a high regard. This was to prove fortunate since in later years she was able to provide Ouspensky with considerable assistance in the administration of his groups in England and America.

* * *

What we know of Ouspensky is very much derived from his writings which, of course, are the outcome of his Damien side, but his Peter side with its love of art and beauty and its delight in good food and wine was always present beneath the surface, particularly on more relaxed occasions. He always had the greatest respect for women, whom he treated with great kindness and consideration throughout his life. The evidence indeed suggests that his relationships with women were severely discouraged by Madame, which prevented him from developing his emotional side as fully as he might have done.

His affections found some outlet in his love for animals which he expresses in his alter ego, Ivan Osokin. He was fond of horse riding and many years later at Lyne Place he was to be seen riding around the estate on his favourite horse Jingles. He was also very fond of cats and when, in 1921, he went to England at the invitation of Lady Rothermere he almost immediately established a favourite cat in residence which, it is said, used to accompany him at his meetings. Cats, he said, were creatures of unusual intelligence, possessing an astral body, and thereby capable of development. This would account for the reverence in which cats were held by the ancient Egyptians.

Throughout his life, therefore, there is this constant interplay between Peter and Damien. His role, to which he dedicated himself from the age of thirty, required the predominant use of Damien, but Peter was always present even though he was not allowed to develop fully. One sometimes wonders what would have happened if he had been allowed greater opportunities.

4

St. Petersburg

In 1909, after the return from his travels, Ouspensky moved to St. Petersburg, the then capital of Russia on the shores of the Baltic 350 miles north-west of Moscow. After the revolution in 1917 it was renamed Petrograd and the seat of government transferred to Moscow, but at the time in question St. Petersburg was both the national and the cultural capital of Russia and with the Academy of Sciences and the State Public Library containing over three million books it provided both the climate and the facilities which he needed for his research.

He renewed his journalistic contacts and gave a number of public lectures on his experiences. It is, indeed, an interesting aspect of his character that although intellectually he was a man apart, he was no hermit but was a popular figure, often referred to jocularly as 'Ouspensky Fourth Dimension'. His lectures attracted large audiences, sometimes of more than a thousand, and this ability to organise public meetings, or inspire others to do so on his behalf, was very valuable to him.

His main occupation at this time, however, was the completion of the philosophical treatise which he had started some years previously. The fresh ideas and experiences gained during his travels provided the inspiration which had been lacking and the work was finished by 1911 and published in 1912 under the title *Tertium Organum*. This, he said in the foreword, was the third canon of thought, following the *Organon* of Aristotle and the *Novum Organum* of Bacon. It was published in an English translation by Claude Bragdon in 1922, since when there have been several editions and fresh translations, the latest (1950) by Madame Kadloubovsky who was his secretary in England for many years.

The book is a feat of intellectual lucidity, not easy to summarise because of the very magnitude of its scope. The early chapters are an objective assessment of the ideas of Hinton and Kant, but he then goes on to show that the fourth dimension, so cosily wrapped in mystery, must not be considered as merely an additional aspect of conventional space. It should be regarded as applying to a realm which *embraces* the phenomenal world, but which cannot be comprehended by the logic of the senses. Hence the necessity for new patterns of thought, into which he endeavours to lead the reader by various extrapolations from conventional thinking.

For example, he says that animals lack concepts. They have perceptions but are unable to collate them into a significant pattern. He cites the case of a cat whose seven kittens became scattered and who was quite unable to reassemble them all in the same place because it could not remember where it had put them. It is not an entirely convincing example because animals do develop simple and sometimes surprising forms of memory. There is the case of a dog who was treated at the People's Dispensary for Sick Animals for earache. A fortnight later it arrived at the Dispensary with a kitten in its mouth; and the kitten was found to be suffering from earache!

However, such instances are examples of instinctive memory. Man is distinguished by the possession of an intellectual mind which enables him to reason. He can develop more comprehensive patterns of association, but even so the concepts which he creates and uses are normally all derived from habitual and stereotyped thinking and hence are of limited significance. Only if he can stretch his mind to think beyond his ordinary attitudes can he begin to develop the full potentialities available to him.

St. Petersburg

This need to think beyond conventional ideas is, in fact, the theme of the whole book. The treatment is intellectual and requires attentive study in relatively small doses. Yet there are occasional flashes of insight, as when he speaks of the expansion of the moment by a four-dimensional consciousness which will be aware of the past, present and future all together as a unity.

There is an exposition of outstanding quality in the chapter on Love which he says is normally completely misunderstood. Hindu mythology regards it as the other face of death. *Siva*, the god of the creative force, is also the god of death and destruction, while his wife, *Parvati*, the goddess of beauty and love is also *Kali*, the goddess of evil and misfortune. Love, he says, is a cosmic force of much greater significance than the physical attraction which Nature uses to maintain the continuity of the species. Gurdjieff used to speak of three types of love. There is physical love which depends on type; emotional love which is unstable and turns into its opposite; and conscious love which is compassion.

There is behind this chapter, and in several other places in the book, a vision of a Universe of great majesty and beauty which he was not able to express explicitly. Perhaps this is why he later called it a terrible book and advised his pupils not to read it, but in fact it was a work of considerable stature and when ten years later it was translated into English it was received with acclaim and was responsible for his introduction to the Western world.

* * *

During his travels he discovered theosophical literature the publication of which was forbidden in Russia at that time. This contained ideas with which he found himself intuitively in accord, for whereas conventional philosophies envisage the Deity by inference from the knowledge of the phenomenal world, theosophy regards the Universe, in all its aspects, as emanating from a supreme but uncreate Source or Godhead. With this, man is able to communicate to a limited extent by the use of his intuitive faculties, transcending the logic of the senses. This idea is the basis of the Kabbalah and even earlier systems, and was interpreted practically in mediaeval times in the mystical sayings of Meister Eckhart and Jacob Boehme.

In more recent times it was expounded by Helena Blavatsky, the daughter of a noble family of Mecklenberg which had settled in Russia in the mid-nineteenth century. Her book *Isis Unveiled* attracted great attention by its startling theories of the evolution of humanity and religion. She was able to demonstrate the use of higher forms of consciousness which aroused great scepticism among those who did not want to believe in anything higher than themselves. In 1875 she formed in New York the Theosophical Society which now has branches all over the world.

Ouspensky recognised the validity of the basic ideas but had reservations about their application. The customary interpretations, he felt, were too facile, an exercise of idle imagination with insufficient emphasis on the need for individual effort. Nevertheless the ideas opened up new horizons for him. He began to realise the existence of esoteric influences through which real knowledge could be transmitted by intelligences of a higher order, influences which were the true inspiration of religion and mysticism and which, by the grace of God, continued to be available despite the gross misinterpretations of arrogant humanity.

According to Madame Blavatsky's original statements the true wisdom is transmitted from time to time by adepts or 'mahatmas' who appear in different parts of the world but are in spiritual communication with each other. By reason of their superior consciousness they can use the body as an instrument of higher intelligence and hence create supernatural manifestations. Her own inspiration, she claimed, was derived from such a group in Tibet.

One can see in retrospect that Ouspensky was at that time an adept in the process of developing, albeit probably unaware

St. Petersburg

of the fact. One is apt to assume that hierophants enter the world fully equipped with spiritual powers. History shows that this is not correct. They have to begin their lives as ordinary mortals but because they have preserved some memory of their origin they are able, by work on themselves, to use their experiences to develop their latent faculties. Ouspensky possessed in remarkable measure this single-minded sense of purpose which guided him throughout the role which he had to play.

* * *

Now that *Tertium Organum* had been completed he began to collect ideas for a further even more comprehensive work which had been in his mind for some time. This was to go beyond the mathematical treatment of his previous works and to be more concerned with an esoteric approach. He realised that all ordinary knowledge is based entirely on the evidence of the physical senses. The information which they provide is interpreted by processes of reasoning which may be relatively simple in matters of everyday life or very profound when it is concerned with the physical laws which govern the behaviour of the familiar world.

Yet throughout the ages there has existed the belief in a knowledge of a different quality concerned with the much larger world beyond the perceptions of the senses. All ancient philosophies and religions speak of this real world but because it is by definition a realm of a different order it is assumed that it must be incomprehensible to ordinary human intelligence. However, legend speaks equally firmly of 'hidden' knowledge which is communicated by a higher intelligence to those who can learn how to listen. This is *esoteric* knowledge, meaning 'from within', and the greater part of this is concerned with the education of the mind to interpret what is being said.

Thinking along these lines Ouspensky had come to believe that many occult writings and symbols were really records of hidden knowledge left by conscious men and hence it was important to discover how these could be properly interpreted. He began to re-examine occult literature from this angle and made a study of the various forms of Yoga. He also investigated the symbolism of the ancient Tarot cards, used ostensibly for fortune telling but actually having a much deeper meaning, which he discussed in a book published in St. Petersburg in 1913. He regarded this, however, as of minor importance, because the material was later incorporated in his second major work, *A New Model of the Universe*, published some years later.

He was aware, however, that a purely intellectual approach would not suffice. Moreover, he felt that the written word, whether philosophical or esoteric, could be no more than a guide to an understanding which has to be acquired by individual effort. He therefore began to conduct a variety of experiments to try to experience higher levels of consciousness for himself. These he subsequently described in the *New Model* in the chapter entitled 'Experimental Mysticism'.

He found that these states could be induced by sitting in a relaxed position, alone, and withdrawing the attention from all the things with which it was normally occupied. The process can be assisted by deliberately placing the attention on different parts of the body in turn. This can create an awareness which is not only of immediate importance, but can accompany the subsequent daily activities not in an obsessive sense but as a feeling of inhabiting the body and looking out upon the world through the senses. (This was often remarked by his pupils who said that he always seemed to know what his body was doing.)

There has to be complete absence of expectation which could only lead to imagination. Indeed, the most significant feature of these more conscious states was that he had no recollection of them on his return to the normal condition. There were, however, certain feelings of which some memory lingered. One was a feeling of wholeness, a feeling that at the higher level everything was connected. A further partial recollection of great interest was that in these more conscious states the feeling of 'I' had no meaning. He had a feeling of the presence of something which he could only call 'not I'. This he felt was his real self, whereas the self of his customary state was entirely imaginary.

Similar experiences have been recorded by other experimenters and it is possible to induce such states by the use of narcotic or psychedelic drugs. Ouspensky said that this was permissible only if it were employed as a conscious exercise, but he stressed that the use of drugs to satisfy a craving for the unusual is very dangerous because it can upset the delicate balance of the body's chemistry. Moreover, it is useless because, as Ouspensky emphasised more than once, one is not allowed to retain the benefit of any super-conscious experience unless it has been paid for in advance by conscious effort.

The principal difficulty with these experiments, however, was that he found he could control nothing. Sometimes illumination came, at other times terror. He realised that guidance is necessary to build a satisfactory bridge between the visible and invisible worlds, and he recalled that there were said to be Eastern schools of Yogis or Sufis wherein suitable methods had been preserved. Did these schools still exist, and could they be penetrated?

He decided once again to set aside his writing and go in search of this hidden knowledge. His travels took him to Egypt, Ceylon and India (where he met Mrs. Annie Besant, the President of the Theosophical Society at Adyar in 1913). He had intended to extend his search into Persia, but the outbreak of war in 1914 caused him to curtail his travels and he returned to Russia by a roundabout route through London (where he made contact with a possible publisher), finally reaching St. Petersburg again via Norway and Finland in November 1914.

Here he had to readjust himself to the conditions but fortunately these were not initially greatly disturbed and he was able to continue with the book on which he had been working, with the added insight gained from his travels. Perhaps his most significant discovery was that esoteric schools did actually exist though not in the form he had expected. There were religious schools of a devotional character, which he could have found in Russia anyway. There were philosophical schools with a shade of asceticism like those of the followers of Ramakrishna and others, which he said were attended by nice people but not possessing real knowledge. There were schools based on the cultivation of trance states which he could not trust since they savoured of spiritualism and self-deception. All demanded dedication and withdrawal from life. There should, he felt, be schools of a more rational type wherein a man had the right, up to a point, to know where he was going.

In particular, he felt that a genuine school would in some way be in spiritual contact with the schools of the past – the schools of Moses and Pythagoras, of Egypt, of the builders of Notre Dame and so forth. This would be contact with the miraculous; but it could not be sought in these terms, since this would only lead to imagination and dreaming. There must, he felt, be techniques of approach which were essentially practical, while still acknowledging the existence of higher levels of intelligence, but these he had so far been unable to discover; yet within a year he was to find what he had been seeking on his own doorstep.

5

Interlude

Ouspensky returned to Russia in a strange frame of mind. Everything had changed with the outbreak of war and he realised why he had felt during his travels an uneasy sense of urgency. He had not found what he sought and he came back with the feeling that what he was looking for would after all be found in Russia herself – as in fact was to be the case, for shortly afterwards he met Gurdjieff.

Meanwhile there was nothing to be done but wait. The war seemed to be having little effect on life in St. Petersburg. He was living in a flat on the Nevsky Prospect, a fashionable quarter similar to London's Piccadilly. This was the centre of the artistic fraternity of the time, a coterie of writers, painters, musicians and actors who would congregate in the evenings after the theatre performances were over in a café called The Errant Dog. Here one would often find Ouspensky in company with his cronies discoursing on the mysteries of time and consciousness far into the night – often not returning home until the dawn was breaking over the Neva.

He started to work again on the book and wrote a chapter on his travels under the heading 'In Search of the Miraculous' – a title which was used many years later for the now familiar book published after his death in 1947. He also completed a chapter on 'Christianity and the New Testament' in which he emphasised that the Gospels were not historical documents but were storehouses of esoteric knowledge and should be interpreted as such.

The Fates, however, were working behind the scenes and the pattern of his life was to change dramatically; but first they gave him an interlude of unexpected delight. At a meeting of the Theosophical Society he met a young woman, Anna Butkovsky, who knew of him but did not recognise him until the person in charge of the meeting asked him if he would say something about the development of the higher faculties as practised by Eastern schools; but he declined, saying that his ideas were not yet adequately formulated and he preferred not to comment.

Anna took the opportunity to talk with him afterwards and he told her that his refusal to comment had been an excuse, because he intended to leave the Society whose members were just sheep, showing no evidence of independent thought; and although he had been invited to join their 'inner circle' with the promise of enlightenment not accessible to the rank and file, he felt that there he would only encounter bigger sheep.

She asked him if he was contemplating a successor to *Tertium Organum*, which she had read with great interest. He did not answer directly but questioned her about her aims and finally invited her to meet him the next morning at Philpoff's café which was close to both their homes. When she arrived she found him already there drinking strong coffee 'à la Varsovienne' for which apparently there was a standing order, because as he finished one cup it was automatically replaced with a fresh one.

They began to discuss his writings and he told her that even before *Tertium Organum* he had contemplated a book with the tentative title 'The Wisdom of the Gods' but had abandoned it because he felt quite unequal to the task of conveying adequately the enormous scope of such a treatise. However, he was working on another book which he hoped to finish shortly.

They began to meet at Philpoff's every day. Ouspensky, then in his late thirties, was clearly uplifted by the companionship

Interlude

of this young woman whose conversation did not merely reflect his own thoughts but contributed complementary ideas of her own. They were both concerned with the possibility of finding a teacher who could instruct them in the practical attainment of real consciousness, and he welcomed her presence because, as he once told her, she was impelled by a will to seek and find which most other people did not possess.

She was a very accomplished pianist, studying at the Conservatoire, and was very sensitive to what she felt was a magical quality in music, expanding the mind and feelings beyond the affairs of everyday life. This excited Ouspensky very much and he asked her to play for him which she did several times at her father's house, and this moved him profoundly. He recalled the Russian fairy story of the Firebird, a bird which always evades capture but in escaping drops a feather from its glowing tail which leaves an indelible mark on the hand of its would-be captor.

A few months later he came to her in some excitement to say that he had at last found the teacher whom they had been so long awaiting. This was the strange mystic, Gurdjieff, whom he met in Moscow (as is described in the next chapter). When Gurdjieff came to St. Petersburg later Ouspensky took Anna to meet him and they had a number of discussions together.

Shortly afterwards, however, the relationship appears to have run its course. In retrospect it seems that the octave had been completed. One of the most practical ideas which Gurdjieff brought from the East was that progress in any development is not uniform but proceeds in a succession of seven steps at each of which there must be a certain accumulation of energy before progress can continue. Moreover at a certain point the momentum slows down and some additional reinforcement or shock is required. If this is available the progress continues, culminating in the achievement of the objective. This, with the seven intervals, forms the pattern of eight 'notes' constituting an octave.

If the interplay of the forces has been correct the result has a certain permanency. In life many octaves fail to be completed usually because the requisite shock is not provided at the appropriate point, and in human relationships this may cause frustration or bitterness. In the present instance, however, the conditions appear to have been right so that each derived a lasting benefit and when the time came they went their separate ways with no demands or regrets. Ouspensky's forebodings of impending changes urged him to complete the work he had on hand while there was yet time. Anna herself had to concentrate on the preparation for her forthcoming examinations at the Conservatoire, and in the ensuing years her contact was with Gurdjieff rather than Ouspensky.

Nevertheless, while it lasted it was a very happy relationship, providing a renewed stimulus to his emotional faculties which had become overshadowed by his exceptionally keen intellect. In an account of the period which she wrote many years later she says in a most moving reference to a conversation between them,

> I remember that in saying all this Ouspensky spoke very quietly, as if talking to himself, and behind his face I suddenly saw another, more radiant countenance filled with a youthful happiness which perhaps no-one but myself ever witnessed. When in later years we were to meet again in Berlin, in Paris and London, he had developed a hard outer shell, and I wondered then why he had crushed the gentle, poetic radiance of his St. Petersburg days. Possibly he thought of this side of himself as a weakness, yet it was in this happy mood that his inspiration and vision were strongest; the intellect had nothing to do with it.
>
> Anna Butkovsky-Hewitt, *With Gurdjieff in St. Petersburg and Paris*

Superficially this may seem a pity, and it is easy to criticise him for his apparent inability to free himself from his intellectual

Interlude

shackles; but to understand him one must realise that throughout his life he was governed by his *daemon*, which in Greek mythology was the attendant spirit charged with steering the individual in the role which he has to play. In the present age of materialism esoteric truth can only reach the majority of people through the intellect and Ouspensky's formulations supply this need to a superlative degree. In these expositions, however, he had of necessity to adopt a remote and impersonal manner because this was what was expected of him. Yet in his more personal contacts he displayed an unforgettable warmth of understanding.

* * *

Meanwhile, spurred on by the sense of urgency, he worked on the completion of several unfinished manuscripts. One of these was a book which he had started earlier containing two short stories. The basic theme of both tales was the trouble which man brings on himself by his constant attitude of expectation. In the first story, The Inventor, the hero frets over the fact that no-one will take up any of his several inventions. Feeling that his life has been wasted he determines to commit suicide and goes to a gunsmith's to buy a suitable weapon; but having looked at several models he perceives an improvement which would revolutionise their effectiveness. He finds a friend who agrees to make his improved gun. It has little success at first until by accident it catches on and orders pour in, only now he finds himself in the power of a real devil – the unceasing pursuit of ever further success.

The second tale takes the form of a conversation with a devil. Devils are commonplace in Russian folklore and are not necessarily evil, so Ouspensky uses the idea as a means of airing his theories. The Benevolent Devil who provides the title for the story explains that his principal function is to try to keep mankind happy by releasing it from the illusion of a superior world. This he says is responsible for all the misery and unhappiness in life, and he has at his command an army of devils employed in trying to dispel this belief. The treatment was amusing but immature and Ouspensky regarded it more as an exercise in writing than a serious contribution. Nevertheless it was published in St. Petersburg in 1916, under the title *Talks with a Devil*. It remained forgotten until after his death when his former pupil J. G. Bennett arranged for it to be translated and published in England in 1972.

Ouspensky's main preoccupation at that time, however, was the completion of the treatise on which he had been at work intermittently ever since the publication of *Tertium Organum* in 1912. This new book was a comprehensive work of over 500 pages which he called *A New Model of the Universe*. It adopted a different approach from his earlier work, being concerned not with the formulation of erudite mathematical concepts but with the development of a proper psychological approach to the problems of science and religion.

He first establishes the existence of esoteric knowledge, i.e. the hidden knowledge emanating from higher levels of the Universe which transcends the logic of the intellectual mind, and then shows how this real knowledge can be applied to provide more meaningful interpretations of the familiar world. He discusses the nature of man's true evolution, which is not concerned with physical stature but with the development of superior qualities of consciousness that are able to communicate with higher levels of intelligence. The subsequent subject matter is wide-ranging and includes chapters on Christianity, Yoga, the Tarot Cards, Dreams, Hypnotism and Eternal Recurrence. He includes details of his experiments in inducing higher states of consciousness and accounts of his world-wide travels in search of hidden knowledge.

Despite the pressure of events he managed to complete the work before the collapse of the regime in 1917 and it was duly published the following year. It was to be many years before it appeared in the Western world, but an English translation was published in New York in 1931 followed by a London

Interlude

issue in 1934, since when it has run through many editions.

The book is indeed a classic, a work of outstanding quality, not merely in respect of the lucidity of thought and exposition but because of its emotional content. It was to be the last of his own writing because shortly after its completion he met the Caucasian mystic George Ivanovitch Gurdjieff who was to have a profound influence on his life. Gurdjieff's ideas provided new dimensions of understanding which supplied answers to many questions which had been in his mind for years and he wrote no more for a long time while he studied the practical interpretation of the system.

When he did again begin to write, his work had the same outstanding lucidity of expression but he was almost entirely concerned with the interpretation and preservation of the teaching which Gurdjieff had introduced. There was no longer the innocent originality of his previous writing and there are those who regret that his genius had not been allowed to fulfil its early promise.

Ouspensky was essentially a man who made things possible. Many people are emotionally aroused by the writings of poets or mystics and endeavour to develop their understanding accordingly. But this is only possible to a very limited extent because the quality of esoteric truth cannot be assimilated by any extension of conventional intellect. It is necessary to find *for oneself* a suitable teacher, either in human guise or by studying the legacies of ancient knowledge in various forms of objective art or music. In either case the inspiration will involve ideas of a new order quite beyond the interpretations of habitual thought.

In the absence of an acceptable teacher (whom he had yet to meet) Ouspensky travelled extensively in the East and was rewarded by a variety of unexpected ideas, which he records in some detail in the book, admittedly without fully understanding them. A particularly striking example is his account of the impressions received from the Sphinx in the Egyptian desert which he records in detail.

Ouspensky: The Unsung Genius

The Sphinx, he says, is indubitably one of the most remarkable of the world's works of art. It was created long before the earliest of Egypt's dynasties, themselves seven thousand years before the birth of Christ, and it has long been considered to be what is, in effect, a book in stone containing the totality of ancient knowledge, a cipher which many have attempted to read. He does not pretend to solve the riddle himself but he records the unexpected and rather terrifying influences to which he was subjected by its presence.

To quote briefly from his comments he says

> When I first read about it I felt that to approach it would require the full equipment of a knowledge different from ours, some new form of perception without which it would be impossible to discover anything from it. But when I saw it for myself I felt something in it that I had never read or ever heard of. . . . The face of the Sphinx strikes one with wonder at the first glance. It is a modern face with little of ancient history about it, except for the head dress. I had thought that it would be an 'alien' face but this is not the case. It is disfigured by the erosion of time, but if you move away a little a kind of veil falls away and there emerges a simple human face with eyes which look beyond you into the unknown distance.
>
> I began to feel a vague and growing uneasiness. I felt that the Sphinx was not seeing me, and not only did not, but could not see me. Not because I was too small and insignificant in comparison with the profundity of wisdom which it contained and guarded. That would have been natural and comprehensible. There was a sense of annihilation, of feeling myself too transient for the Sphinx to be able to notice me. If I were to stay there indefinitely my whole life would flash by so swiftly that it would not see me. I did not, and could not exist for it. Which prompted the terrifying question – do I exist at all, even for myself?
>
> The thought of Eternity flashed into my consciousness,

Interlude

inducing an icy coldness. All my ideas about time and about life were becoming confused. I felt that in these moments when I stood before the Sphinx it lived through the events and happenings of thousands of years, and that on the other hand centuries passed for it like moments. How this could be I did not understand. But I felt that my consciousness grasped perhaps the shadow of the exalted fantasy and clairvoyance of the artists who had created it.

This kind of inspired narrative is typical of the humility of Ouspensky's genius which permitted him to experience brief moments of higher consciousness. *A New Model of the Universe* was written in draft before he met Gurdjieff and it is fortunate that he did not attempt to update it because although he was later able to formulate a comprehensive structure of a Universe embodying a succession of levels of intelligence and consciousness it lacked the vivid sense of wonder of his early writings.

6

Meeting with Gurdjieff

Early in 1915 Ouspensky came across an article in a Moscow paper about a ballet called 'The Struggle of the Magicians', said to have been arranged by a certain Hindu mystic. He was not much impressed for he had seen various 'sacred' dances during his travels and had no reason to suspect that this was of special interest. He was engaged at the time with a series of lectures in St. Petersburg about his travels which, despite the war, were attracting large audiences and he received many letters and personal visits from people who, he felt, were no longer able to accept the customary forms of lying on which so-called civilisation is based.

He was encouraged to repeat these lectures in Moscow, at one of which he was approached by a colleague who told him of a group which was studying occult philosophy directed by a Caucasian Greek named Gurdjieff, who was in fact the 'Hindu' mystic responsible for the ballet of the magicians mentioned in the newspaper article. Ouspensky was still not impressed for he had encountered many pseudo-mystical groups whose 'revelations' were no more than imagination. People invent miracles for themselves, he said, invent exactly what is expected of them in a mixture of superstition and auto-suggestion.

Hence it was only after the persistent effort of his colleague that he agreed reluctantly to meet this character, which he did in an unpretentious and rather noisy café frequented by small-time business representatives and agents. Here, seated by himself at a small table drinking coffee, was the man they had come to meet. Ouspensky later described him as a man of middle age with a black moustache and piercing eyes, who gave the curious impression of being in a disguise which you see through and yet have to pretend that you do not. He spoke Russian badly with a strong Caucasian accent, but his utterances in any case were brief and laconic.

It was to be a momentous occasion. From the very first moments of their meeting Ouspensky recognised Gurdjieff as a man of superior stature, the teacher whom he had so long been awaiting, and knew intuitively that here he would find the answers which had so far eluded him. They spoke of his travels, of esoteric legend, of yogi schools, and in particular of a school in India which studied the chemistry of the body in a manner which could change a man's moral and psychological nature.

Gurdjieff agreed that there were such schools but said that they used the methods in different ways and not always correctly; but he implied that if Ouspensky joined him he would learn more about it. The discussion naturally turned to the subject of drugs and their use in inducing higher states of consciousness. Gurdjieff said again that this was a method which had its uses but was often misapplied. It can sometimes confirm, he says, that something which a man has arrived at theoretically actually exists, so that he knows for the first time where he is going and what he has to work on; but in general the proper use of narcotics involves a detailed understanding of the chemistry of the body and must only be undertaken under the direction of experienced teachers. Without this direction a man may attain exceptional powers, but they do not last and he ultimately goes mad; so that one must exercise great caution in such matters.

All this interested Ouspensky very much for it dealt with things which had been on the fringe of his understanding for many years. He was invited to attend a school which was operating nearby, where he met a small group of young intellectuals. However, when he tried to talk to them about their activities their answers were evasive, using strange and unintelligible terminology. They spoke of work on themselves, though failed to explain in what way, and he felt a disappointing barrier either of unintelligence or deliberate reserve.

The impact of Gurdjieff himself was quite different. This man possessed undeniably unusual qualities. Yet even so there was something uncomfortable about him. He had spoken of the expenses involved in organising a school, yet both the location and the furnishing of the room where they had met were far from impressive. He had said that his work had attracted the attention of a number of well-known professors and artists, but of these there was no sign whatever. Yet despite this and the discouraging response from the pupils he had met, Ouspensky says that all the time Gurdjieff produced in him an unexpected desire to laugh and sing, as though he had escaped from some strange prison.

As it happened there was always to be this feeling of unease between them for though their spiritual aspirations were in harmony there was a certain clash of personalities. Gurdjieff was an opportunist who had no compunction in adopting any means which furthered his ends, as he himself shows in his book *Meetings with Remarkable Men*. Ouspensky's aristocratic upbringing had imbued him with a sense of propriety and integrity which he had, to some extent, to discard. Gurdjieff said that Ouspensky listened to his head whereas he himself listened to his heart, which was something Ouspensky would have to learn to do.

He did not visit the group again, but met Gurdjieff every day in the same café for the ensuing week, during which time he learned more about this strange man and his system of ideas. Gurdjieff reverted to the matter of the expense involved in running a group and said that each of the members was required to contribute 1000 roubles a year to the funds. When Ouspensky suggested that this seemed excessive, and that in any case he doubted whether they would be able to pay, Gurdjieff said it was necessary because by reason of their nature his groups could only be small. He himself could not, and ought not to, bear the expense personally, and in any case people did not value a thing if they did not have to pay for it. (Much later, when they had fled from Russia after the revolution and were finding conditions very hard he reminded Ouspensky of this conversation, pointing out that if he had not collected what money he could in Moscow it would have been difficult to continue the teaching. But in one way or another there was always sufficient to keep going, and as conditions became more stable some of Ouspensky's influential contacts provided considerable funds.)

At the end of the week Ouspensky said that he had to return to St. Petersburg because he had several books in preparation and wanted to discuss them with his publisher. Gurdjieff said that he would follow him shortly and intimated, without saying it in so many words, that he would welcome him as one of his pupils if he so wished. With characteristic integrity Ouspensky said that he would only accept the invitation on clearly defined terms. In particular he could not agree to any obligation of secrecy. Ideas might emerge about such matters as time or higher dimensions which he had studied for years and he would have to feel free to ponder on these for himself.

Gurdjieff said that some restraint was essential because there were some matters which could only be properly spoken about by initiates. Ouspensky agreed and said that if the requirement of secrecy was imposed simply to prevent the transmission of ideas in a distorted form then he could accept it and certainly would not write anything until he had fully understood it.

He asked further if there were any conditions attached to the joining of a group. Was a man tied to it or could he leave at any time if he wished? Gurdjieff said there were not, and could not be, any obligations, because man in his customary condition does not know who he is and is quite incapable of making any permanent commitment. He cannot even keep secret what he hears until he has developed some coherent consciousness so that people are not told anything significant until they can be trusted.

With these assurances Ouspensky agreed to join him and for the next eighteen months he saw a great deal of Gurdjieff and began to absorb, little by little, the startling new ideas which were being discussed. With his penchant for documentation he kept a record of his many conversations with Gurdjieff and other members of the group. This was not with any intention of publication but to clarify his own understanding. However, they were to prove very valuable many years later when he collated them in his book *In Search of the Miraculous* which is recognised as the authoritative exposition of Gurdjieff's teaching.

* * *

As Gurdjieff's ideas began to take shape in his mind he realised how completely they complemented his own earlier thinking. In many respects they involved a complete reversal of the conventional approach. Most important was the concept that the Universe was a living and evolving structure created by a Supreme or Absolute Intelligence in a succession of increasingly detailed stages of which the physical world is nearly the lowest. Each of these levels has its own intelligence and consciousness, again of descending order, the whole structure being continuously enlivened by energy devolving from the Absolute.

As a corollary of this concept it is clear that the higher states of consciousness about which people are wont to speculate vaguely are not mere extensions of ordinary awareness but are manifestations of the superior intelligences in the already existing structure and hence, as Ouspensky himself had found in his experiments, are of an entirely different order.

This cosmological hierarchy, however, was initially discussed only as a background to the more immediately practical aspect of the teaching, which was that man's usual so-called consciousness is an illusion. His behaviour is that of a machine which reacts entirely automatically to the stimulus of life events in accordance with 'programmes', or patterns of associations, which have been built up by education and experience. This the group was told to observe and verify for themselves, for it was an axiom of the system that nothing was to be believed without question. Only when one has established the truth of any statement for oneself can any real understanding develop.

Finally, there was the clear distinction between the spiritual and temporal parts of a man (or woman). Each has its own reality but they are of a different order. The spiritual part, which is unmanifest, i.e. not evident to the physical senses, originates from a very high level in the Universe, but in the course of its development it has to adapt itself to progressively lower levels of existence until, in the condition which Gurdjieff called Essence, it inhabits a physical body.

This body is a remarkably intelligent structure which is provided for the purpose of making significant use of the experiences of life by developing the patterns of associations which constitute the Personality. This activity should be consciously directed, but in the usual state no such direction is present and the body operates entirely automatically for its own gratification.

Ouspensky found this philosophy completely acceptable, and over the years he was able to establish the validity of the ideas for himself not only in the psychological aspects but also in its cosmological implications, which accorded well with his concepts of worlds of higher dimensions. In particular, it gave him an insight into the place and purpose of man in the Universe, involving a clear and unsentimental obligation which he had not been able to discern in conventional religion.

* * *

In the autumn of 1915 Gurdjieff came to St. Petersburg regularly and talked to groups which Ouspensky had assembled for him. Despite the troubled conditions of the time there began to develop the nucleus of an esoteric school which operated for the best part of a year. However, this was interrupted towards the end of 1916 when Ouspensky was called up for service in the Guards Sappers, which he described as a strange but not unpleasant experience. It did not last long because after only four months he was discharged on account of his poor sight. A fortnight later, in March 1917, the Czar Nicholas II abdicated and a revolutionary government took over.

This appeared to be the climax of the unrest which had been brewing for so long. Ouspensky said that it marked 'the end of Russian history' and he decided to leave the country as soon as possible and spend the rest of the war in some neutral territory. Gurdjieff had already left for the Caucasus but it was not until October that Ouspensky was able to clear up his affairs and make his own escape. It was, he said later, quite impossible to stay there any longer. There was a sickly expectation of something inevitable. Nobody understood anything. He finally left St. Petersburg for the last time on October 15th, a week before the Bolshevik revolution.

7

The Caucasus

The winter of 1917 held little promise of comfort. Apart from the difficulty of the 1000 mile journey from St. Petersburg the conditions in the Caucasus itself were even more bleak. The Bolsheviks were in possession of the northern and western territory but the southern part was a melange of separate states each with its own laws, its own police and its own prices, each trying to defend its autonomy and involved in addition with the armies still trying to oppose the Bolshevik regime.

For Ouspensky it was a period of great difficulty. His established sources of revenue were gone, at least temporarily. Prices were unstable and rising daily, already inflated one hundred-fold and often more, on top of which bribery on an unprecedented scale was necessary to obtain anything important. The wages of workers had increased roughly in keeping with requirements but cultured people were unable to command such increases and life became very precarious. Ouspensky wrote at the time that he was alive only because his boots and trousers still held together. When they disintegrated he expected that he would follow suit!

In the event, he managed to survive and began to re-establish some journalistic activity. In particular, he was able, through the assistance of a British observer, C. E. Bechhofer, to establish contact with A. R. Orage who was the editor of *The New Age*, a literary and cultural weekly paper which had a wide circulation in England at the time. For this he wrote a series of articles which described in graphic terms the chaotic conditions. These have recently been reissued under the title *Letters from Russia 1919* and make interesting, and in many respects prophetic reading today.

In one of these he expounds what he calls the Law of Opposite Aims and Results. Everything, he says, leads to results contrary to the original intention. The war with Germany which had been undertaken with the object of destroying militarism, had turned back on its course and resulted in the overthrow of the monarchy. The idealistic revolutionaries had never intended to create the conditions in which Bolshevism could flourish, and so on. (Later he was to realise that this was another example of the octave pattern mentioned in Chapter 5, in which the development goes astray if the original intention is not reinforced by a suitable shock at the appropriate point.)

In September 1919 he writes that he has obtained some English newspapers for the first time in two years and is appalled by the fact that they do not seem to know anything. They do not see the harm being done to civilisation by Bolshevism and suggest that the Western world should accept and even encourage the regime. In reality, he says, Bolshevism is not a political system but a doctrine of plunder aimed at the destruction of all freedom. Do you make friends with a burglar or an assassin?

The articles are lucid and objective, with little reference to his personal privations. Yet from some comments by Bechhofer in an epilogue one has the impression that Ouspensky was waiting, living each day as it came, until a clear direction emerged. This was one of his strengths, this ability to wait for the right moment. Often in private conversations he would maintain a discussion, perhaps beyond the point of physical weariness, until suddenly conditions became right and a significant step forward was possible.

* * *

The Caucasus

In the early stages of his exile he had lost touch with Gurdjieff, but finally met him again at a place called Tuapse on the shores of the Black Sea, an industrial town largely centred round an oil refinery. Here he learned of an experiment which had been made at Essentuki some miles to the north where Gurdjieff had collected a dozen people who worked for six weeks under the rigid disciplines of a school. The experiment was by way of a try-out, abandoned as suddenly as it had begun, and he was now trying to establish a centre under less arduous conditions at Tuapse. He concocted a letter which he persuaded Ouspensky to send out over his own signature to all the people who had been concerned in the groups in St. Petersburg and Moscow and ultimately some forty people were assembled to start a group there. It was not run on such rigid lines as the Essentuki experiment but was still subject to school disciplines and involved a variety of practical activities, including the rehearsal of rhythms and dances based on Dervish routines which Gurdjieff had observed during his travels, and had been demonstrated for a time in Moscow.

These exercises are an important part of school activities. They involve movements of the body and limbs different from and additional to those which are employed in ordinary activities. For example, one foot may be pointed to the front, side and rear in succession while an arm may be required to perform some quite unrelated movement, with perhaps the head turning in opposition to the arm movement. All this requires a directed attention, difficult to remember and even harder to sustain. Yet it is an exercise which induces a state of awareness which is curiously exhilarating. Gurdjieff devised a number of these exercises, performed to strangely moving music which he himself had composed, and these movements and their music have been preserved in schools today.

Ouspensky lent what support he could to these activities, though they were evidently tentative and he hoped that in due course a more secure base for the operations would emerge. He knew that any genuine efforts to raise the level of consciousness would attract esoteric influences which in their own time would provide what was necessary. As was said to the children of Israel in a similar time of tribulation, 'In every place where My name is caused to be remembered I will come among you and bless you.' (Exodus xx, 24.)

Meanwhile, however, it was becoming increasingly important to establish a measure of life stability. The Caucasus was still in a confused state and he moved south into Turkey where he was finally able to find accommodation on the island of Prinkipo some ten miles south-east of Constantinople (now Istanbul) in the Sea of Marmara. Here he was at last reunited in more secure conditions with his wife Sophie Grigorevna and the two children of her former marriage. (He never had any children of his own.)

Gurdjieff in the meantime was exercising his entrepreneurial talents in a variety of ways, one being as a seller of carpets, and as usual making money at it, as he describes in *Meetings with Remarkable Men*. Ouspensky's sober attitudes caused him to regard these opportunist activities with some distaste and he himself had to earn his living the hard way, which he did by teaching English to Russian evacuees and mathematics to children. His book *A New Model of the Universe* had been published in St. Petersburg in 1918 despite the troubled conditions, and this began to bring him some extra revenue.

He began once again to hold meetings though he had difficulty at first in finding a suitable venue. However this was solved by a certain Mrs. Beaumont who had a large house in Pera, a district of Constantinople, and made available one of her rooms for regular Wednesday meetings.[2] When he was asked what these were about he used to say that they were concerned with the Transformation of Man, the theme being that man's true evolution was not a development of his ordinary physical and mental faculties but involved a change of state. This was

The Caucasus

very much in line with the ideas of higher-dimensional worlds which he had discussed in his books long before he met Gurdjieff.

He spoke at times about Gurdjieff's classification of the different types of men and women. It is evident that people are by no means all the same. There are many variations of character, differences of race or creed, or environment, all of which influence the behaviour. Ouspensky said that all these distinctions were of secondary importance and that the real classification was determined by the predominant characteristics. These fall into three main classes which he called Number 1, 2 and 3 Man rsepectively. Number 1 Man is principally concerned with movement and instinctive behaviour. People of the second type derive their meaning mainly from their emotions, responding to impressions of art and music, while the third category is chiefly intellectual, making its judgments in terms of thought and reason. Everyone reacts in all three ways to a varying degree but it is the predominant characteristic which determines their type, and it is clear that this kind of classification is independent of race or nationality. Moreover, because of the basically different approach to situations these different types do not understand one another, as is depicted in the legend of the tower of Babel, in which the lack of understanding arose not from differences of spoken language but of type.

None of these three types is inherently superior. They are all incomplete in that they are one-sided, and a basic requirement of conscious living is the cultivation of a balanced psychology in which all three functions are equally developed, producing what Ouspensky called Number 4 Man, Balanced Man. He is still not a conscious individual but has the basis of becoming so, and hence is sometimes designated Transitional Man.

Any further evolution can then only be in a different direction involving higher orders of consciousness, so that he postulated three further types, Numbers 5, 6 and 7 Man of ascending quality as shown in the diagram below.

| 1 Instinctive Man | 2 Emotional Man | 3 Intellectual Man | 4 Transitional (Balanced) Man | 5 Integrated Man | 6 Conscious Man | 7 Perfected Man |

It was a concept which he amplified later, but always with the proviso that it was an idea to be understood emotionally without attaching undue significance to the numbers. On one occasion a pupil asked in tones of awe, 'Are you a Number 6 Man?' to which he replied with a twinkle in his eye, 'Why so low?'

* * *

Early in 1921 he received three copies of the American edition of *Tertium Organum* which had been translated into English by Claude Bragdon. This gave him great pleasure, particularly as it was accompanied by a substantial royalty cheque, which he felt would at last enable him to travel to England as he had long wished to do.

Almost simultaneously he received a telegram from New York signed by Lady Rothermere saying, 'Deeply impressed by your book Tertium Organum. Wish meet you New York or London. Will pay all expenses.' He inquired about her from J. G. Bennett who was in Constantinople at the time and finding that she was the wife of one of London's Press Barons he accepted the invitation subject to the provision of the necessary permits and visas. After several weeks these duly arrived and Ouspensky left with his wife and family for London, where another adventurous chapter was to begin.

8

London

The meeting with Lady Rothermere marked the beginning of a new era in Ouspensky's life. He was then 42 years old and of authoritative stature. His new-found sponsor was able to introduce him to a number of influential people, including Ralph Philipson, a Northumberland coal owner who, with his Russian-born wife, became keenly interested in the ideas. Arrangements were made for him to give a series of lectures to the Quest Society which attracted considerable attention. He spoke of the morass of complacency into which mankind had strayed. Because of the comprehensive library of associations which man acquires by education and experience he is able to interpret and make intelligent use of the multitudinous impressions received by his senses every moment and this creates the illusion that he is fully conscious. Actually he is not in command of his faculties to more than a minimal extent. His behaviour is that of a machine which responds automatically and without significant variation to the impact of events as interpreted by the firmly established associations of habit.

This has two disastrous effects. Because of this blind self-satisfaction he is unable to understand his fellow men, let alone his real situation. His meaning is derived almost entirely from the gratification of personal demands, the pursuit of which breeds the violence and crime of modern civilisation. The second and more significant result is that because of this surrender of his true potentialities he fails to fulfil the purpose of his creation, and becomes a thing of no account, serving only the cosmic requirements of the earth, likened by Christ to the chaff which is cut down and cast into the fire.

Strong meat. Yet such was the climate of disillusion in the aftermath of the war that there were many who had ears to hear; and for these Ouspensky held weekly meetings at a house in Warwick Gardens which had been placed at his disposal. Kenneth Walker, the distinguished surgeon, describes in his book *Venture with Ideas* his early impressions of these meetings. He had decided to attend with some misgiving, for there were at that time various pseudo-mystical groups in operation; but he was persuaded by his colleague Maurice Nicoll to go, and found his way to a dimly-lit house where, in company with two others, he was welcomed by a pleasant lady of Russian extraction who ticked their names off on a list.

Inside was a small room furnished with a large number of chairs facing a table with a blackboard nearby. Gradually the room filled up. There was no talk. Everyone, he says, sat in a state of anticipation like a Scottish congregation awaiting the minister, but there was no sign of Ouspensky though it was well past the scheduled hour. Suddenly a door opened to admit a very solid man of medium height and close-cropped grey hair who sat down at the table, peered at some notes through some very strong glasses, looked at the audience for the first time and said, 'Well?'

It was an unexpected entry. Kenneth Walker says that he had anticipated an obvious mystic. The man in front of him looked anything but that – a scientist, perhaps, or a lawyer – someone with his feet firmly planted on the ground. Yet when, after a brief silence, he began to talk, his stature immediately became apparent. He used no gestures but made his statements bluntly with no attempt to convince his audience. One had the feeling that he was simply concerned to present a number of ideas about which his hearers could make up their own minds.

This, in fact, appears to epitomise the very essence of Ouspensky's approach. Nothing, he said, was to be accepted without question; it has to be verified by each individual for himself. The validity of the psychological formulations can be confirmed by simple self-observation, though this is not easy because of the burden of self-esteem which we acquire from childhood. Anything which offends this image of ourselves is either rejected or justified, but if one can observe objectively, without criticism or judgment, it becomes possible to understand what is really happening.

This is the meaning of the inscription at the entrance to the temple of the Oracle at Delphi – Know Thyself – an injunction which is usually interpreted very superficially, as if it were easy to do. In fact it requires considerable time and honesty but it can raise the whole level of one's Being. This is a significant idea. We are accustomed to refer casually to ourselves as human beings, usually with the arrogant implication of superiority over all other animals. But everything has its Being, which defines its essential nature, and its place and purpose in the Universe, and it is clear that there can be different qualities or levels of Being. A stone in its natural state is simply part of the earth's crust, but if it is worked on by a craftsman it may become useful as building material or possibly sculpted into an object of beauty. In either case its level of Being is increased. The Being of a man or woman is similarly capable of transformation if it can be subjected to the right influences, and according to some authorities the full text of the Delphic inscription read, 'Know thyself, and thou shalt understand the Universe and God.'

The cosmological aspects of the teaching are clearly not so easily validated. They postulate a Universe of great majesty and intelligence vastly greater than the egocentric concepts of materialism, and one has to adopt a complete reversal of conventional thinking. All esoteric legend speaks of a created universe emanating from a Supreme Being, as is said succinctly in the opening words of the Old Testament, 'In the beginning God created the heaven and the earth; and the earth was without form and void.' This is followed by an allegorical description of the way in which successive levels of order were introduced.

The cosmology which Gurdjieff brought from the East formulates this succession in a manner which is not only comprehensible and acceptable to modern scientific thought, but contains the deeply meaningful concept of a structure which manifests the will of the Supreme Being in a series of stages of increasing complexity and decreasing intelligence. The lower levels of this structure are within the range of physical perception with which man is normally content. But he possesses a range of little-used paranormal senses which can comprehend the potentialities of the higher, but unmanifest, levels. These are the higher-dimensional worlds which Ouspensky had postulated long before he met Gurdjieff, as regions obeying laws of a superior order and yet comprehending and embracing the lower levels. As man's consciousness develops, these intuitive faculties provide increasing illumination of the real situation and his place and purpose therein.

This understanding, however, cannot be achieved directly but only through the patient effort to increase one's level of consciousness, which can only start from knowledge of oneself. Hence Ouspensky's early lectures were principally concerned with extremely practical psychology. Kenneth Walker records that the first meeting which he attended discussed the idea of the many 'I's' in one's personality.[8] All one's awareness of the world is derived from impressions received by the physical senses. These are intrinsically purely objective and isolated items of information which can convey no meaning until they are correlated into a connected pattern. This the brain does by the use of associations stored in the memory as a result of which the information becomes meaningful and appropriate action is possible.

These increasingly numerous associations resolve themselves

London

into small groups having appropriate relevance to particular types of event. All one's ordinary thoughts, feelings and actions are determined by the operation of these well-established 'behaviour units' with which we identify ourselves and say I to. A more conscious man would not accept these automatic responses without question, but would exercise discrimination, replacing the customary interpretations by associations of a different quality concerned with real values instead of the gratification of desire.

The realisation of one's dependence on these independent and unco-ordinated personalities dispels the illusion of the single and permanent I which one calls oneself and believes to be in command of the situation. If the real state of affairs can be observed *and accepted* it becomes possible to begin to exercise a conscious control of the activities which can lead to the state of what Gurdjieff called 'self-remembering'.

Such was the aim of the weekly meetings at Warwick Gardens, interspersed occasionally with talks on one of the cosmological aspects of the teaching. They were mostly conducted by Ouspensky himself though sometimes they were opened by one of his more senior pupils who would ask for questions which Ouspensky could answer when he arrived.

In the early days, stringent secrecy was imposed. Attendance was only by permission and one was not allowed to talk about the ideas outside the meetings. Cars had to be parked in side streets away from the actual meeting place. This was due in part to Ouspensky's native caution, but mainly to avoid attracting undue attention and to preserve the ideas from degradation by insufficiently-informed discussion. Later as the regime became established it was possible for these conditions to be relaxed, and to speak openly of the teaching usually referred to as the System, or more succinctly as the Work, because its basic tenet was the necessity for effort.

9

The Prieuré

While Ouspensky was organising his meetings in London, Gurdjieff was in Germany, attended by some of the members of his group from Turkestan. When he heard of the activities in England he came to London and was introduced by Ouspensky to his group. Dr. Nicoll describes this first appearance in his diary.[7] The group, awed by his presence, with Ouspensky beside him as interpreter, sat petrified in silence until someone timidly asked, 'Mr. Gurdjieff, what would it be like to be conscious in Essence?' Briefly and laconically he replied, 'Everything more vivid.'

He said no more on that occasion, but he did make several further visits, remaining in London for about two months during which there was some talk of trying to find a suitable house in the country where group work could be started in a school atmosphere. However, early in 1922 Gurdjieff heard about a large property in Fontainebleau which it seemed might become available. It was called the Château du Prieuré, formerly the home of Madame de Maintenon, then in the possession of the widow of Maître Labori, the famous advocate in the Dreyfus case. It was a large house standing in 200 acres of ground and had earlier been a Carmelite monastery, so that both by its situation and its history it was eminently suitable for a school.

It was some time before the purchase could be completed,

The Prieuré

which was made possible only by generous contributions from Lady Rothermere, Ralph Philipson and other members of Ouspensky's group, but in October Gurdjieff obtained possession and started what he called The Institute for the Harmonious Development of Man.

Here some sixty students took up residence. They were of varying nationalities; English, American, a few French and many Russians from Gurdjieff's former groups, all of whom under his direction embarked upon a wide variety of activities. One of their first tasks was to reassemble a surplus aircraft hangar which had been delivered to them (in pieces) free of charge by the French Government. This was to serve as their Study House in which they held their meetings and rehearsed the dances similar to those which had been organised at Tuapse. There was also the acquisition and housing of a variety of livestock to help the larder.

It was a spartan existence, as is recorded by various people who took part in the adventure, notably by J. G. Bennett who was there from the beginning.[1] Among others who were present was Maurice Nicoll, who had sold his lucrative Harley Street practice and lived for two years at the Institute with his wife and baby daughter.[7] They were joined by other well-known people including Katherine Mansfield and A. R. Orage, who sold his journal *The New Age*, to the consternation of literary London, in order to take part in the experiment. In due course, they were joined by Ouspensky himself, with his wife and family, though Ouspensky did not remain permanently but returned to London from time to time.

After the initial flurry the real object of the exercise began to emerge. There were talks in the Study House by Gurdjieff, difficult to follow because of his Caucasian accent and often lasting far into the night; but though these contained the most luminous ideas, they were only part of the activities which were constantly imposed to permit the development of unfamiliar and unused faculties with the aim of becoming 'balanced man'. Yet even more important were the continual assaults on the False Personality, the self-pride and vanity which, like two giants, stalk before us and arrange all that we do.

Gurdjieff's blunt and often savage rudeness left no room for self-esteem. All one's ordinary values were ruthlessly demolished. Here, as he loved to say, one could learn to be an idiot. In conventional parlance the word has the connotation of not being in one's right mind. But if by 'right' mind one is referring to the established usage of habit, then a conscious man is indeed an idiot, for the mind which guides his behaviour is entirely superior to that which controls his mechanical existence. The Greek word *idios* means 'one's own' so that an idiot is a man who is in possession of himself.

Hanging from the ceiling round the walls of the Study House were a series of aphorisms written in a curious Caucasian quasi-Arabic script of which English translations have fortunately been preserved. One of these, of peculiar significance, read:

> Always remember that you are here having already understood the necessity of contending only with yourself. Thank everyone who affords you the opportunity.

To contend with oneself is a most difficult exercise. We are accustomed to contending with other people, or with situations. The very word implies strife, the attempt to impose our will on other people sometimes violently, usually more subtly by playing on their foibles. At the same time, we ourselves are imposed upon. People continually make demands on us to which we may or may not submit but will almost certainly resent. Gurdjieff often spoke of the need to tolerate the unpleasant manifestations of others.

To contend with oneself is a different matter. It involves seeing that all these problems are of one's own making. It is I who make the demands – on other people, on the world, on the whole Universe; and no one I, but whichever of the

The Prieuré

hundreds of I's in myself happens to be on stage at the moment. How can this motley collection contend with itself? As Juvenal asked in Roman times, 'Quis custodiet ipsos custodes?' Who is to guard the guards themselves?

A new will is required, operating at a higher level which can see behind the facade of the Personality – a term itself derived from the Latin *persona*, meaning a mask. This more conscious entity can observe the varied aspects of behaviour without judgment or criticism and can recognise their relative value. Those I's which could help one's inner development can be nourished. Those which are useless can be starved so that they lose their power and we become free.

* * *

In this atmosphere of the surrender of false values it was possible for Gurdjieff to speak of matters of larger scale, which he did at length when the occasion was propitious. He spoke of the Universe as a living structure brought into being by the Absolute or Supreme Intelligence through the operation of two fundamental laws – the Law of Three and the Law of Seven. The first of these is implicit in many esoteric and religious legends. It states that for any effective manifestation three forces are required. The first is the active force conveying the intention. This is automatically opposed by a second force of opposition – as in the well-known scientific dictum, to every action there is an equal and opposite reaction. But this is a condition of stalemate, and if there is to be any result a third or reconciling force is necessary in order that the other two forces may be brought into a practical relationship.

The Law of Seven is not so well known. It is the basis of the octave structure already referred to earlier and is concerned with the way any succession of events must be related if there is to be a successful outcome. The progression is represented by the seven notes of the major musical octave which was devised by an early esoteric school to illustrate the process; and its significant characteristic is that there are two points where the progress temporarily slows down and may even lose direction, so that some additional reinforcement is required if the development is to succeed.

These two laws, and their appropriate inter-relationships, are discussed in detail by Ouspensky in his later books *In Search of the Miraculous* and *The Fourth Way*. Even a partial understanding of their action provides a greatly enriched meaning not only of the Universe itself but in the day-to-day trivia of life.

* * *

From time to time Gurdjieff would expand these ideas to speak of the place and purpose of man in the cosmic pattern. Man, he insisted, was not a mere accident but had been created as a self-developing organism to refine, by individual effort, certain psychological energies which were needed by higher levels in the Universe. But in the growth of materialism man had forgotten his obligations and unless he could be awakened the results could be disastrous. Esoteric teaching is concerned to remind man of his true purpose, but in the present era of chaos, the age of Kali-yuga or barbarism foretold in legend, the return to sanity is an increasingly urgent necessity.

However, everything changes in cosmic time and the requirements change accordingly. This earth does not exist in isolation. It is affected by planetary and stellar influences which are not constant but vary with the slow transit of the whole solar system through the heavens. This is a recurring transit which occupies what is called the Great Year amounting to 25,800 earth years, during which period it passes in succession through the twelve divisions or signs of the ancient Zodiac which were originally named after the constellations which occupied a central position in each division.

These extra-terrestrial influences are partly physical but

The Prieuré

mainly psychological. The physical effects are known to science. The psychological influences are not so well known. Their study is part of the ancient science of astrology which has today been largely superseded by the materialistic science of astronomy. The effect of these influences is really part of genuine occult knowledge, and if properly interpreted they could have a significant impact on events. The so-called astrology of the media today is, of course, a mere travesty of the art to cater for popular superstition.

The transit through each sign occupies about 2000 years, during which both the nature and the circumstances of humanity slowly change. Hence it is necessary that the form of esoteric influences should be modified accordingly, as is confirmed by historical record. At the present time we are approaching the end of the age of Pisces, the fishes, which runs from AD 1 to AD 2160, and has been influenced by the teaching of the great initiates of the period, Christ, Buddha and Mohammed. Previous ages have been similarly inspired by great religious leaders speaking the language of their time.

The developments of the present century both in its technology and the rapidly expanding population of the world necessitate new methods. We are in a period of transition from Pisces to Aquarius. Traditionally in the Age of Pisces the truth is hidden, to be revealed only through love. In the coming Aquarian age there will be more open vision, to be understood by the development of consciousness. It will not, we are told, be characterised by a new Messiah but by small groups conducted by adepts who have themselves achieved a measure of enlightenment.

There is a record of an interesting dream by one of Ouspensky's pupils which illustrates this situation. Dreams are of two types. Ordinary dreams, many of which are not even remembered, are merely fantasies created by the undirected brain, often triggered by some suppressed anxiety. But during sleep (and sometimes at other periods when the Personality is quiescent) the mind can receive ideas from higher levels of intelligence which the brain then interprets in some form of symbolism.

In the dream in question the person was attending a circus at the Albert Hall when suddenly all the animals ran amok and began to attack the audience. Then all the lights went out and chaos reigned; but slowly little pinpoints of light appeared throughout the auditorium and peace was restored. The riot of the animals clearly represents the present state of violence, the age of Kali-yuga, but by many small individual efforts the situation will be remedied.

Gurdjieff and Ouspensky, each in his own way, were the precursors of this coming age of Aquarius. They have left us signposts to this new territory which are being followed by increasing numbers of people.

10

The Break with Gurdjieff

Ouspensky provided considerable assistance in the establishment of the Institute at Fontainebleau. Not only did he obtain substantial financial support from Ralph Philipson and other influential people but he urged those of his group who could do so to take the opportunity of joining Gurdjieff at the Prieuré, as he himself proposed to do. It seems probable that he saw this new venture as providing the possibility of the stable headquarters for the teaching for which he had long hoped.

In the event this was not to be. Work continued at the Institute for barely two years under intermittent direction, for Gurdjieff often had to be away on fund-raising expeditions, and Ouspensky had to return to London frequently to maintain contact with his group. In retrospect, however, it is clear that it could not be a permanent and cloistered community because its whole object was to educate its pupils in the development of conscious participation in the events of everyday life.

Traditional ways of seeking enlightenment involve withdrawal from life to work in seclusion on some particular aspect of one's nature, and there are three recognised approaches. The first is the way of the fakir who seeks mastery over his instinctive-moving functions. The second is the way of the monk who seeks to refine his emotional faculties, while the third is the way of yoga which is concerned basically with the development of intellectual power. Gurdjieff's system constitutes a fourth way, which seeks to develop all three faculties to an equal and harmonious extent. It is the way of Number 4 Man from which development can begin in a different (spiritual) direction, and this of necessity involves living in life and learning to use the varied experiences as opportunities.

The system, indeed, became known as The Fourth Way. It is the most fruitful, and the most rapid, of all the ways, though this must be understood in a cosmic rather than personal connotation. According to esoteric teaching the conscious participation in an event transforms the quality of the energy which it contains, and this refined energy nourishes Essence which thereby begins to fulfil the purpose for which it is created. However, if only one type of activity is developed the process is incomplete and a further endeavour is necessary to develop the other two faculties. This will clearly be a prolonged operation, necessarily involving a succession of lives. The development of all the faculties simultaneously permits a much speedier fulfilment of the cosmic purpose even though this may still require more than one life for its full achievement.

Thus by its very nature the journey on the Fourth Way cannot be completed by indefinite residence in a school. Nor is it possible to make more than a token start by perfunctory attendance, sitting at the feet of a master and waiting for enlightenment. As Gurdjieff expressed it in his laconic way, 'Institute hatching place for eggs. Supplies the heat. Chicken must try to break shell. Then help and individual teaching possible.' The Prieuré, he said, provided excellent opportunities for the development of consciousness, but people forgot why they had come and became identified with everything.

After a time some of the people began to see this for themselves and realised that if they were to continue on the path it would be necessary to leave the Institute, if only for a time, and go back into life, but with the object of using their experiences consciously. One of these was Dr. James Young, a colleague of Maurice Nicoll, who left to resume his practice;

The Break with Gurdjieff

another was A. R. Orage, the distinguished former editor of *The New Age*, who left for America in order to re-establish himself in the literary world. This he achieved with distinction and in the meantime he organised a flourishing group of his own which prepared the way for a very successful visit by Gurdjieff in December 1923.

Maurice Nicoll had to return to England in 1923 to attend the funeral of his father, Sir William Robertson Nicoll, who died in May of that year.[7] He was occupied for several months in clearing up his affairs, but in August he rejoined his wife and family at the Prieuré. He records in his diary that even this short break increased his evaluation of the system and made him better able to bear and understand the disciplines imposed, and he remained until the Institute was unexpectedly closed late in 1924.

The most surprising departure, however, was that of Ouspensky. His wife and family had been resident from the beginning but he himself had only attended intermittently and in January 1924 he returned to London and announced that he had decided to break his connection with Gurdjieff and operate independently. This caused considerable consternation because for years they had been regarded as inseparable allies in the promulgation of the teaching.

Yet for some time Ouspensky had been finding himself out of sympathy with Gurdjieff. He believed whole-heartedly in his ideas, but did not approve of his methods which he regarded as too autocratic. People were being asked to accept what they had not understood. This to him was anathema because in his view the essence of the teaching was that it left a man free to make his own choice. He said that this admittedly involved a certain risk, and even danger, since the freedom could be misunderstood and wrongly used; yet it was the only valid method because consciousness cannot be imposed by force, nor developed by following any restrictive system.

Many people have criticised this break with Gurdjieff, which they interpret as a display of typical Russian arrogance; but this is judgment without understanding and the real situation involves much deeper consideration. The truth is that although it appears that Ouspensky made this momentous decision himself, and may possibly have believed so at the time, it was actually made for him by his *daemon* in fulfilment of the role he had to play.

There is a quite unjustified belief that Gurdjieff could do no wrong. His spiritual stature was outstanding and he had clearly achieved a high level of consciousness; but he had nevertheless to inhabit a physical body, with its concomitant Personality, and while he had learned to contend with this there were many aspects of his behaviour which were far from saintly. Middleton Murry, the husband of Katherine Mansfield, described him as a man of violent temper, greedy for money, personally lustful, extravagant and boastful.

One might regard this as a biased judgment since Middleton Murry's wife, who had long been suffering from TB, was unable to withstand the rigours of the regime at the Prieuré and had died there. Yet in fact it was fair comment. All these characteristics were indeed present but Gurdjieff had learned to subordinate them to his aim, which was the development of consciousness both in himself and his pupils.

This subjugation of the Personality is illustrated in a legend from the Talmud about the patriarch Moses, which Ouspensky quotes in *A New Model of the Universe*. The world was enthralled by the miracle of the Exodus and the name of Moses was on everyone's lips. The king of Arabistan summoned his best painter and commanded him to go in search of Moses and bring back a portrait of him. When the painter returned, the king submitted the painting to his most skilled sages and asked them to deduce the qualities of this remarkable man, and the source of his power.

To his astonishment they said that this was the portrait of a cruel and haughty man, possessed by the desire for power and all the vices which exist in the world. This the king could not believe, so he decided to visit the camp of Israel himself. When he arrived he saw that his painter had portrayed Moses faithfully, but having seen the man himself he immediately recognised his outstanding stature, and concluded that his sages were utterly incompetent in their judgments. 'Not so', said Moses. 'Both your painter and your sages are right. All the vices of which your wise men spoke have been assigned to me by nature. But by long and intense efforts of will I gradually overcame them so that all that opposed them became my second nature; and in this lies my greatest pride.'

This is conscious behaviour, which does not involve the elimination of unpleasant characteristics but deprives them of their power; so that they become subject to the direction of real will and may even be used in the furtherance of a conscious aim. In the Work this is called the way of 'Sly Man'. A direct approach to any objective inevitably attracts difficulties, which may be tedious and even insurmountable. Sly Man uses the situations themselves to attain the result by using the difficulties as opportunities, not hesitating to adopt any kind of trickery if necessary. There is an amusing tale that Sly Man once met the Devil in a tavern and they got into conversation. The Devil was disconsolate because human beings were rapidly losing their souls. How then could he lead them to perdition? Hell was practically empty. Sly Man was very sympathetic and plied him with drinks to cheer him up, until he became so drunk that the Sly Man slipped out of the tavern and left the Devil to pay for the drinks.[5]

Gurdjieff was a master of these tactics. He made shameless use of Ouspensky from their first meeting, recognising the value of his keen intellect and literary expertise. He believed that he had a mandate from his Sufi school to arouse humanity from its state of sleep and in pursuit of this aim he had no compunction in making statements which were blatantly untrue and generally using methods which by ordinary standards were fundamentally dishonest. He used his Personality to the full in the cultivation of a far from benevolent despotism, for kindness was a characteristic entirely lacking in his make-up.

Ouspensky's cultured and gentle upbringing and his ingrained sense of integrity could not tolerate this behaviour indefinitely. It savoured too much of personal ambition, which was not altogether untrue because Gurdjieff's sense of urgency drove him to many ill-considered actions. If we are to understand these two men we must realise that each had his role to play – roles which in the sight of Heaven were complementary, even though apparently antagonistic at life level.

Ouspensky has been called the Plato to Gurdjieff's Socrates. Certainly his genius for lucidity of expression enabled him to convey the practical aspects of the teaching to a much wider audience than Gurdjieff himself was able to reach, and for this posterity has reason to be extremely grateful. Socrates is variously regarded as a mystic, a sceptic or a complete atheist. Whatever the truth, he influenced people profoundly by the way he spoke to them about themselves; and the same could be said of Gurdjieff. But such influence is personal and those that come after have to be shown how the principles can be applied in practice.

Ouspensky, then, had to leave Gurdjieff. Their continued association would have damaged what they both believed in. It was a lonely path for him to follow because Gurdjieff never communicated with him again and often vilified him to other people. But Ouspensky remained faithful to what he believed to be his obligation to the Work, which he pursued steadfastly, and in the ensuing years he grew steadily in stature.

* * *

The routine of the Prieuré was violently disrupted in July 1924 when Gurdjieff, who had only recently returned from his visit

The Break with Gurdjieff

to America, had a serious car accident, running off the road into a tree at 60 miles per hour. He was seriously injured and for a time his life was despaired of. He was clearly unable to supervise the affairs of the Institute so that in November it was closed down and all the pupils, except for a few intimates, were scattered.

Ultimately Gurdjieff recovered, but he regarded the incident as indicating that this phase of his work was finished, and he decided to devote himself to writing in order to perpetuate the ideas in his mind while he still could. Hence he began to put together (on many scraps of paper written in pencil) an allegorical narrative purporting to be tales told by Beelzebub to his grandson concerning a number of visits made to Earth, and the curious creatures which populate it. Beelzebub explains that the Universe is a vast structure of transformation wherein everything is food for something higher. Man's function is to provide a certain kind of transformation which would serve the cosmic process and at the same time provide him with the material from which he could organise an astral body. However, the Controllers of the Universe were afraid that man might not be willing to accept this obligation indefinitely, so they equipped him with imagination which caused him to interpret everything in terms of his own importance and well-being. However, this proved to be too powerful a hypnotic, so that it became necessary to provide esoteric teaching whereby he could be reminded of his true purpose.

He speaks of other ideas of which traces exist in occult literature, such as the possible existence of higher (unmanifest) bodies in man. The first (physical) body disintegrates at death, but a man can during his lifetime organise three higher bodies of relatively increasing immortality; but he has to know how and be willing to make the appropriate effort.[9] There is discussion on the structure of interrelated cosmoses operating like the 'wheels within wheels' of Ezekiel's vision, and the continuous creation of the Megalocosmos which by the conjunction of the Laws of

Three and Seven maintains a constant replenishment of the Universe.

According to Beelzebub there was one messenger from the Controllers who succeeded for a time in awakening humanity to a state of objective consciousness. This messenger, the Saintly Ashiata Shiemash, taught (to initiates only) that by long heredity Essence has become tainted, so that our innate aspirations are contaminated and produce spurious effects. He taught that man himself contains all the necessary data for self-development, and under his guidance nations, classes and wars disappeared. But after his death all was destroyed by vandals, people of a type all too familiar today which he called Hasnamus, whose chief characteristics include:

1 Every depravity, conscious and unconscious
2 Delight in leading others astray
3 Irresistible urge to kill
4 Enjoyment of what they have not earned
5 Striving to be what they are not

He says, moreover, that Hasnamus characteristics do not necessarily disappear with the death of the physical body but can exist as a powerful force for evil in the world.

This again is a very brief precis of a remarkable book, in the production of which Gurdjieff withdrew himself almost completely, even from his closest associates. Much of it was circulated in draft form among his groups, but it was not generally released until after his death when it was published under the title *All and Everything.*

The style is emotional, full of strange terms and apparent irrelevancies which some people find difficult to accept, still less understand. Many of the statements are elaborate expositions of occult knowledge without any attempt at substantiation. It is knowledge, perhaps, which in olden times would have been kept secret within the priesthood and only communicated to the

The Break with Gurdjieff

initiate after a long preparation. Without this preliminary work the ideas are liable to remain mere fantasy, but if there is already a basis of extraordinary thinking – the *metanoia* of the Work – they can produce a most inspiring and practical understanding. Ouspensky's brilliant formulations provide an invaluable background to Gurdjieff's insight but the full value of the ideas lies behind the words and can only be discerned by the emotional mind which the reader has to apply for himself.

This major work was followed later by two further books which Gurdjieff had written during the same period, intended to complete a trilogy. The first was entitled *Meetings with Remarkable Men* and is basically an account of his early experiences on his travels in search of the Masters of Wisdom. Being mainly a straightforward narrative it is written in a much easier style but it nevertheless contains significant truths if one knows where to look. In 1979 it was made into a film, directed by Peter Brook, which aroused much interest.

The third book *Life is real only then when 'I am'* is an attempt to provide practical instruction in the art of self-remembering. Its style is again peculiar but its message is clear once one has recognised that there is a self to remember – a conscious entity which should be in command of the motley collection of little persons whom we dignify with our name, but which, in the state of sleep, are mere automata brought into operation by the random impact of life events.

I I

London Again

The period following his break with Gurdjieff was one of great difficulty for Ouspensky, the more so since he was not accompanied by his wife who had remained at the Institute. Nevertheless he felt that he had made the right decision and his immediate task was to assemble the principal members of his group and acquaint them of the situation.

To them he explained that the decision was entirely personal. When he had first met the teaching it had been agreed that one must not believe anything blindly, nor do anything which one did not understand, but in later years Gurdjieff had been departing from these principles and was demanding allegiance without question. He said that the activities were tending towards ritual observance which was not the way he personally could accept. The members of the group were free to make their own choice, but if they stayed with him all contact with Gurdjieff would have to cease.

In answer to a question from Ralph Philipson, the bluff north-country coal-owner on whom Ouspensky depended so much, he said that Gurdjieff was a very remarkable man, having potentialities much greater than ordinary people. But he was going through a crisis of internal conflict. We all had many I's, mostly weak so that the constant conflicts between them did no harm. Gurdjieff had only two very strong groups of I's, one good, one bad. He thought that in the end the good would triumph, but meantime it was dangerous to meet him. We could not help him, nor he us. Someone asked what would happen if the struggle went the wrong way. Ouspensky said that in such an event he could go mad, or possibly attract to himself some disaster in which those around him would be involved. This was a strangely prophetic answer in view of Gurdjieff's terrible accident six months later.

Asked whether he regretted having met Gurdjieff he said, 'Never, why should I? I got much from him for which I am always very grateful.' He said that Gurdjieff gave him many ideas which he had not known before, and a new system of thought, of which fragments could be found elsewhere but which had never before been so remarkably co-ordinated. It was the ideas which were important. Their practical interpretation could vary according to the teacher and he felt it important to be single-minded in this respect. He enforced this isolation with what may seem to have been undue severity but his aim was to encourage individual awakening. He always acknowledged Gurdjieff as the originator of the System and discussed his ideas in detail, but while they were re-establishing themselves contact with other groups was forbidden.

He resumed his meetings at Warwick Gardens which were attended by a number of prominent people. He was assisted by various stalwarts, notably J. G. Bennett, who had known him from as far back as the Constantinople days, and Maurice Nicoll who had been with him at Fontainebleau and was to become a particularly valuable aide.

With them he could sometimes have private conversations in which he was able to speak not as a teacher but as a human being with the hopes and aspirations, the doubts and uncertainties of an ordinary man. The role of a teacher is of necessity a lonely one because few people can overcome their (right) awe. Bennett and Nicoll (and later C. S. Nott) were able to talk with him naturally while still respecting his superior stature, and this was a great comfort to him in his task.

Bennett records a conversation with Ouspensky in the little sitting room at Gwendwr Road when Ouspensky said that he was convinced of the existence of a Great Source from which esoteric influences come.[2] He believed that Gurdjieff had made contact with this Source, but it was an incomplete contact. Something was missing which he had not been able to find. Nor had Ouspensky himself had any greater success in his own travels, for it seemed that the Source was better hidden than people supposed. Hence he felt that the only hope was for the Source to find us, which it can only do if we have made ready to receive it. This was why he was giving lectures in London and elsewhere, and trying to preserve the ideas of the System. If those who have real knowledge see that we can be of use to them, they may send someone.

In retrospect, it seems that it was the communication of the ideas which was incomplete, not the ideas themselves. Real knowledge is emotional, concerned with relationships which can only be discerned intuitively and cannot be understood or even adequately communicated in words. But in this material age man's intuitive faculties have become atrophied so that his initial access to understanding can only be through his intellect; but if this is submitted to the direction of his internal mind it becomes possible for help to be received.

The very multiplicity of nations today suggests that this help will not be provided through the advent of some great new religious prophet. The world leaders of today are political and attract fervent support from the masses who are concerned only with material advantage. But behind the scenes there is the leaven of esoteric influences which can flourish in apparently isolated situations where the spiritual climate is suitable, and if the right atmosphere has been cultivated interpreters appear who are inspired by the conscious levels of the Universe where the real leadership lies.

This was Ouspensky's motivation in this third phase of his life, namely the preparation of conditions suitable for the recep-

London Again

tion of conscious influences. With characteristic patience he did not hurry these moves but was prepared to wait until they matured in their own time. Events, he believed, were manifestations of causes existing at a higher level and could only be significantly influenced by an understanding at that level. Without this understanding attempts to modify the course of events only led to confusion and often produced the exact opposite of the desired effect – the Law of Opposite Aims and Results of which he had written in his *Letters from Russia* ten years earlier.

Meanwhile he was occupied with the preparation of an English edition of *A New Model of the Universe*. This had been translated by some members of the group under his supervision and the various chapters were read and discussed at length by the group as a whole to make sure that the translation adequately conveyed what Ouspensky wanted to say. It was ultimately published in New York in 1931 with a second, revised, edition in London in 1934, since when many further editions have appeared.

This book was originally written in 1914 before he had met Gurdjieff and was a work of considerable stature in its own right. Its whole basis is the recognition of the existence of intelligences of a higher order and the consequent development of more meaningful interpretations of the familiar world. As he says in the Preface, the idea of esotericism is chiefly concerned with *higher mind*. The ordinary mind (even of a genius) is not the highest possible. The human mind can rise to levels inconceivable to conventional understanding and we can see the results of such higher intelligence in the Christian Gospels; in Eastern Scriptures; in the Upanishads; in the Mahabharata; in works of art like the Great Sphinx at Gizeh; in great works of literature and music and so forth; but the true valuation of the meaning of such memorials requires training and the development of a perception beyond that of the normal mind.

The preparation of this English edition provided the opportunity for a reaffirmation of his basic understanding, which was useful while his main aim was taking shape. It is often necessary, indeed, to restate what one has previously understood to prepare for further progress. As Meister Eckhart, the 14th century divine, says in one of his sermons,

> Suppose one feels God's spirit is not working in one, but rather that one's inner man is God-forsaken, that is the proper moment for the outward man to exercise the practical virtues, such as are the most feasible and useful to him.
>
> Meister Eckhart, *Sermons and Collations* III, translated by C. de B. Evans.

Ouspensky's 'practical virtues' were pre-eminently his love of writing and his meticulous search for the right phrase. Dr. Nicoll notes in his diary the trouble he took in the chapter on Christianity.[7] He had by him versions of the New Testament in German, French, Russian and English (both Authorised and Revised), and compared the various translations with the original Greek text in order to be sure of conveying the real meaning; and it was part of his remarkable erudition that he was able to understand all these languages which he had learned during his early years as a translator.

One of his most noteworthy interpretations was that of the 'daily bread' mentioned in the familiar Lord's Prayer. The customary translation runs, 'Give us this day our daily bread', usually regarded as a request for enough to eat. Ouspensky pointed out that this had nothing to do with physical food but referred to spiritual nourishment. The word quite inadequately translated as 'daily' (epiousios) has a much deeper meaning implying 'beyond the ordinary' so that the bread requested is nourishment for the mind, provided by a higher intelligence.

Knowing this meticulous care, one has a great respect for Ouspensky's writings. One cannot dismiss a sentence which one does not understand, or agree with, by assuming it to be a poor translation and that he really meant something else.

London Again

His group grew in numbers and in stature. He did not allow it to become too large so that it was possible to maintain personal contact. Those who were present at the meetings reported that they were rich in understanding. He would sometimes give a brief introductory talk but preferred the method of question and answer which he always insisted was more useful. Occasionally he would come into the room and sit down and wait for some observation. If no-one spoke he would say, 'No questions. No meeting', and leave abruptly!

The questions and answers were reported and selections from these records and others were published many years later, after his death, in the book entitled *The Fourth Way*. He would ignore formatory questions, i.e. questions concerned only with detail without awareness of the meaning which these details served. These he would turn back on the questioner or sometimes pretend to be deaf. If someone quoted a remark made on some previous occasion he would say, 'In what connection did I say that?' He always insisted, indeed, that remarks must not be repeated out of context. But questions which arose from attempts to think for oneself always produced a response, often of a depth far beneath the surface.

Meanwhile, he was quietly collating the notes which he had made during his years with Gurdjieff while they were still fresh in his mind. He began to develop the ideas in more detail for in many cases, such as the concept of the cosmoses, the original presentation had been very brief, and this expanded thinking often formed the subject of his talks to the group. It was, in fact, a period of preparation which could best be described as a time of active quiescence.

12

Madame Ouspensky

For the first few years after Ouspensky's return to England his wife remained at the Prieuré and helped to maintain some continuity after Gurdjieff's accident. The Institute was closed at the end of 1924 but a few of the older disciples remained to form a nucleus for renewed activity if and when it was required. However, when after many months Gurdjieff recovered, his outlook had changed. He abandoned any idea of reviving the former regime and told the faithful few that they must leave.

Madame therefore rejoined her husband in London and began to assist him in his work. She was not altogether happy with the situation because there seemed to be insufficient opportunity for group activity. Ouspensky appears to have been lethargic in this respect, having been concerned almost entirely with the reiteration of the ideas of the teaching. Yet he frequently emphasised that while it was essential to acquire a clear understanding of the basic principles of the system, this was no more than the foundation of a structure which had to be assembled by individual effort. However, as Ouspensky often emphasised, this very effort is of a peculiar quality involving what he called a passive mind. In life we make aims of various kinds. These involve active intention which we attempt to implement by the application of our own knowledge and skills. Conscious aim cannot be achieved with this kind of endeavour. It requires the acceptance of, and submission to, the authority of a higher level of intelligence, about which one's ordinary education and experience knows nothing.

Hence this passive mind is difficult to acquire by oneself, nor is it attainable to any significant degree from books or lectures alone. It requires the stimulus of contact with other people who are on the same journey, with whom under the guidance of a teacher one may begin to question the attitudes and opinions of habit and open the mind to influences of a different order.

This is the basis of an esoteric school (of which today there is an increasing number). It may contain as few as ten people or as many as fifty to a hundred. Anything larger is undesirable because of the difficulty of maintaining proper contact. The effectiveness of a group clearly depends on the understanding of the teacher but it is influenced to an even greater degree by the attitude of its members, and if this is wrong the group will fail and gradually disintegrate.

In a note written some years earlier (in 1922) Ouspensky records a discussion on the possibility of becoming a real group. The first requirement, he says, is avoidance of identifying. This is a word much used in the Work to describe the incorrect feeling of 'I' which enters into all ordinary activity. It is important to be able to participate in an event without being involved in it. So he says, 'The first necessity is not to identify with ourselves or each other, and *especially* not with the group.' This involves above all the suppression of self – *not* self-abnegation in any religious sense, but the realisation that the 'I' of one's ordinary desires and intentions is no more than an automaton, of purely transitory importance.

The second necessity is a right attitude to the Work, the understanding that it is a system of ideas designed to produce an increase of cosmic harmony rather than personal advancement. This process requires the development of individual consciousness and the consequent growth of Essence, but this is incidental. It is necessary to recognise and accept this obligation – which is the reason for man's creation – and be willing to take risks and not mind what happens (even to be ready to be turned out of a group for the good of the rest). Such an impersonal attitude could lead to the development of a real group, in which the members would be aware of each other on a level quite above life relationships.

Groups in the Caucasus had failed because of wrong attitude. The members remained intensely identified with themselves – with what they were going to get out of it – and with the group as a kind of friendly society, so that it was not a group at all and melted into nothing; and perhaps with this in mind, Ouspensky had not been in any hurry to start a school in London.

Madame Ouspensky, however, fresh from and experienced in the activities at Fontainebleau, felt that the time was ripe for such a venture. The facilities in Kensington were quite inadequate, so that she began to look around for a suitable place and eventually found a Victorian mansion called Gadsden in Hayes, Kent, standing in some seven acres of ground. It was within easy reach of London and seemed well able to provide the right conditions for group activity, and in due time she commenced work with eight to ten residential pupils, augmented by others who came for one or two days at the weekends.

This led to a certain division of responsibility; Madame concerning herself with practical work, leaving Ouspensky free for teaching and writing. It was an arrangement which suited him well for he was happy to be relieved of the distraction from what he believed to be his main task, the cultivation of a widening atmosphere suitable for the reception of esoteric influences.

Actually, despite the authoritative style of his intellectual address his kindly nature always made it difficult for him to subject people to the blunt and forceful criticism which they might well need. Gurdjieff regarded him as a weak man, and said so in his more arrogant moods, but people have to work with the tools which they have been given, and posterity can be grateful for the outstanding use which Ouspensky made of his literary expertise at this time.

Madame Ouspensky

He was content, therefore, to leave matters of personal instruction to Madame, who by all accounts was something of a martinet. She did not concern herself with teaching, which she did not regard as her role, but she had an awareness of people's level of understanding which enabled her to provide them with the stimulus which they needed at particular times.

Her manner was blunt and rather forbidding, for she also had the Russian authoritarian characteristics – though of a more emotional quality than was the case with Ouspensky. C. S. Nott, a man of varied activities who had worked with both Gurdjieff and Orage, visited Ouspensky at Gadsden with his wife. He describes in one of his books[6] the large drawing room in which they were received, full of beautiful Russian prints and ornaments – everything, he says, very elegant. He found Ouspensky not the cold, severe intellectual he had expected but warm and easy to talk to. Tea was brought in by some of the pupils, during which Madame Ouspensky did most of the talking. At the end she said, 'Ah! I see there are many things you do not understand', and when he mentioned Orage she said that he also often understood things wrongly, and was too formatory. This is a word used in the System to describe the literal yes-or-no interpretations of conventional logic as distinct from real thinking which embraces both opposites together.

Nevertheless this was the beginning of a contact which was to last for many years. He had many conversations with both of them. Madame, he says, was invariably stimulating, though always the Grand Duchess keeping you at a distance, so that he never felt with her the warmth which Ouspensky radiated in his more mellow moods.

* * *

Meanwhile Ouspensky, who had completed the editing of the English translation of *A New Model of the Universe*, which was duly published in 1931, decided to begin work on a third book relating specifically to the ideas of the teaching. Hitherto this had been, and still was, communicated only by word of mouth. This was a deliberate policy because if the ideas were committed to paper and freely distributed they would be no more than a new system of philosophy. If they are to be rightly understood and valued they must be paid for by individual effort beyond a mere perfunctory interest. As Gurdjieff used to say – only super-effort counts.

Nevertheless he foresaw that circumstances would inevitably change. Neither he himself nor Gurdjieff would live for ever, and though they could instruct suitable disciples to carry on the teaching, they in their turn would have to hand over to a further generation; and at each stage some of the original purity of the ideas was likely to be lost. Hence he felt the need to compile an authentic record of the teaching as he had received it, while it was still fresh in his mind.

He was aware that after the recovery from his accident Gurdjieff was devoting himself to writing. But he was not optimistic as to the outcome because he had a poor opinion of Gurdjieff as an author. In any case it seemed that what was emerging was some kind of cosmological allegory so that he felt more than ever the need for a simple and coherent presentation of the practical tenets of the teaching and to this he devoted the greater part of his time at this period.

It was not intended for immediate publication, and in fact did not appear until after his death, and the lack of urgency enabled him to give full rein to his penchant for clarity of expression. He decided that the purpose would best be served by adopting a narrative style rather than a series of lectures, which was a happy choice since it introduced an emotional content into the writing which had been lacking in his earlier books.

He had the advantage of being able to discuss the various chapters with his group, which enabled him to amend the text where necessary to be sure of conveying accurately what was in his mind. Moreover, he was able to expand by his own thinking several of the cosmological ideas, such as the concept of the system of ascending cosmoses, which Gurdjieff regarded as of great importance but had only discussed rather briefly.

The first two chapters are concerned with his own early travels in the pursuit of ancient wisdom and his meeting and preliminary conversations with Gurdjieff, to whom he refers subsequently simply as G. He writes with refreshing simplicity of the extraordinary ideas of which G. spoke – the concept, for example, of the sun, planets and earth as living beings, part of a hierarchy of intelligences, and of man's situation in this structure. Much of this, he admits, he found difficult to accept since it seemed to be mere fantasy without foundation. Yet his intuition knew that the ideas were true and he was prepared to wait until his understanding developed.

He then begins to speak in the same vein of the specific ideas of the Work as postulated by G. such as the idea that man is a machine – or more correctly, that he inhabits a machine, called the body, which is not consciously directed. But instead of expounding this idea as a theory he shows how it can be verified by actual self-observation and cites numerous practical examples of what G. called wrong psychic functions, which he discusses in detail.

He pursues the same tactics in discussing the many other aspects of the teaching, such as the concept of the mind as a multiple structure comprising several divisions or Centres concerned with the different functions of the body; and the concept of different levels of consciousness of which only the lowest is normally used. All these ideas are illustrated by practical interpretations which can be verified for oneself.

He goes on to speak of the cosmological ideas, which treat the Universe as a living and evolving creation. Here he presents the ideas as originally formulated by G. to the early groups and shows how by discussions among themselves they began to understand that these were not expressions of occult philosophy but were inspiring expositions of a real and intelligent structure.

This is no more than a bare outline of a remarkable book running into some 400 pages which sets out in invigorating detail the whole basis of the teaching. Its greatest value lies in the humility of approach which characterises its pages, for he is not expounding from the pulpit but is endeavouring to share with the reader something which has penetrated the very core of his Being, an impression which is enhanced by the concluding chapters which contain an account of some of the early experiences in the troubled days of 1916–17.

Ouspensky had intended to call the book *Fragments of an Unknown Teaching*, for he had always felt that Gurdjieff's formulations were only a partial exposition of the truth, and in the discussions among his group it was always referred to as 'The Fragments'. However, he discovered that his friend G. R. S. Meade had written a book entitled *Fragments of a Faith Forgotten* so he decided to call it *In Search of the Miraculous*, under which title it appeared posthumously in 1950.

Gurdjieff was aware that this book was being prepared, and approved of it. Indeed when he was shown some of the early chapters he is reported to have said, 'Before I hate Ouspensky. Now I love him. This very exact. He tell what I say.'[2] But he insisted that it should not be published before his own book, *All and Everything*. As it happened neither book was published until after their deaths when, happily, they both appeared together.

The book is undoubtedly Ouspensky's finest work, since it develops from emotional perception in his time-body, the pattern existing in the unmanifest world which contains all the events of the life. Ordinary memory is a mechanical recollection by the brain of associations in the so-called past. Real memory is an awareness of various parts of the life simultaneously, together with their interconnections, and is therefore infinitely more vivid. Hence his formulations have a quality of reality far beyond their intellectual content.

13

Maurice Nicoll

Of the many people who attended Ouspensky's meetings in Warwick Gardens there was one with whom he developed a particularly happy relationship. This was Maurice Nicoll, a Harley Street consultant who was one of the earliest exponents of psychological medicine. In his earlier years he had studied under Dr. Jung in Vienna and had developed a freshness of outlook which responded instantly to the ideas which Ouspensky was teaching.

They first met at a lecture given to the Quest Society in 1920, from which Nicoll returned in a state of exaltation, saying that Ouspensky was the only man who had ever answered his questions. His wife, Catherine, said afterwards that he appeared transformed, as though irradiated by an inner light. The lectures were continued privately at a house in Warwick Gardens, and as time developed Ouspensky would sometimes talk to individual members of the group at his flat in Gwendwr Road, where he would often dine with Dr. and Mrs. Nicoll and talk by candle-light far into the night, sometimes in company with Orage, the brilliant editor of the literary weekly *The New Age*.

In 1922 Dr. Nicoll sold his Harley Street practice and went with his wife and baby daughter to live with Gurdjieff at the recently opened Institute at Fontainebleau, to which the Nicolls had made a substantial financial contribution. They took with them a great deal of luggage, anticipating that they would spend the rest of their lives there, but in the event the visit only lasted for some two years, since the Institute was closed in the autumn of 1924. Nicoll then returned with his family to England, where he had to rebuild his practice. For a time conditions were precarious but eventually they established themselves in a house belonging to his mother, Lady Robertson Nicoll, in Frognal, and were able to renew their contact with Ouspensky, who was continuing to hold meetings at Warwick Gardens.

This was the beginning of a most fruitful period for both parties, which was to last for seven years. Nicoll records in his diary that there was a notable difference in the quality of the meetings, for whereas initially the ideas had been conveyed intellectually they now had a vital and living quality which was developing from their practical application. The teaching was no longer theory. It had been transformed into experience.

A very deep personal relationship developed between them. It seemed that Nicoll was the only member of the group with whom Ouspensky could really relax. He said later that this was because Nicoll could speak to him emotionally about the ideas which they were pursuing, and was able more than anyone else to make him laugh. Laughter is not usually associated with the pursuit of higher things, but in fact it is both necessary and valuable. Gurdjieff said that it was Nature's way of relieving us of surplus energy but it can be of different qualities. Mechanical laughter arises from a conflict between opposites, between what one expects and what actually happens. This builds up a tension which the body relieves unconsciously by an ejaculation of air. Excessive and uncontrolled laughter is a clear indication of useless accumulation of energy. Conscious laughter, on the other hand, has a certain quality of joyousness which arises from seeing both opposites together and pupils were often reminded of Plato's dictum that serious things cannot be understood without laughable things. A conscious man, perhaps, will have no need of laughter but for ordinary mortals it prevents one from being too heavily identified with a situation.

Maurice Nicoll

Ouspensky had a highly-developed capacity for inner separation. He could be aware of events but not involved in them, and by this understanding was often able to release unnecessary tensions in other people. In one of his Commentaries Dr. Nicoll refers to occasions when he used to go to Ouspensky to have a private and serious conversation and found himself being regarded with an amused and almost beautiful expression while he said, 'How, Nicoll? What do you want to say? Have another glass of Montrachet.' By which time, of course, he had been lifted into another state in which the dark and heavy thoughts that belong to the general idea of being serious were gone.

One can see how Ouspensky enjoyed Nicoll's companionship, partly because Madame, his wife, had decided to remain at the Prieuré for a time and he welcomed a kindred spirit with whom he could communicate. On one occasion he asked Nicoll what his aim was. Nicoll said that he would like to have the power of feeling meaning in all the experiences he had had. 'I am sure', he said, 'that you remember your life far better than I remember mine, and that your life has had more meaning.' Ouspensky replied, 'Yes, but not quite in the way you mean. As a child I did not play with toys. I was less under imagination and saw what life was like at a very early stage.'

Nicoll said that he had never thought of life as needing to be thought about, but had taken it all for granted, to which Ouspensky remarked, 'Yes, that is why it had little meaning for you. You were simply carried along by it, to some imagined clear goal. It is only when you realise that life is taking you nowhere that it begins to have meaning.' This is a strange idea, which one tends to interpret as something to be dealt with in the future – possibly in a recurrence of the life. Actually one's whole life can be enriched with meaning now – and only now.

One incident early in their relationship is of particular significance. At Warwick Gardens Ouspensky would often arrange for one of the senior pupils to open the meeting with a view to creating the right atmosphere and perhaps formulating some questions which the Master might speak about when he came in. When Nicoll was first asked to open the meeting the following week he gave a good deal of thought to the matter, wishing to prepare an opening worthy of the honour. When he arrived, however, he was told that after all he would not be needed and that Ouspensky would take the meeting himself. This was a typical test of a kind often contrived in school work to see whether he could accept this cavalier treatment without rancour, but more to show that his earnest preparation had been made from a wrong place in himself. A 'Work' meeting is not a lecture but has to have a quality of asking, of request to a higher level.

To Ouspensky's delight Nicoll understood and when some years later he was authorised to teach his own group everything he did was always guided by this inner acknowledgement of a higher authority.

* * *

In 1927 Dr. Nicoll rented a seaside property called Alley Cottage at Sidlesham in Sussex. Here in the spring and summer months Mrs. Nicoll used to reside with the family, joined by Dr. Nicoll at the weekends. It was surrounded on three sides by marshland and the sea came up twice a day to the garden wall. It was an excellent location for relaxation and they were joined almost every other weekend by Ouspensky, sometimes accompanied by Madame who had by then returned from Fontainebleau.

It was evidently a very happy time, as Mrs. Pogson, Dr. Nicoll's secretary, records in her biography of the family.[7] There were long walks, sometimes occupied with conversation, but often in silence, and there were frequent visits to the local pub, The Crab and Lobster. Sometimes there would be dinners by candlelight at Alley Cottage, at which Ouspensky would reminisce on his homeland, this vast country capable of engulfing a dozen British Isles; a country of many districts each with its own culture, so that Russia had its own England, Wales, Scotland and Ireland.

Dr. Nicoll made many notes in his diary about these times, and the visits they made to surrounding places. He was clearly feeling himself in the role of page to his master, for he never lost his deep respect for Ouspensky. This is in refreshing contrast to many other writers who secretly believe themselves to be equal to him in stature and criticise with neither love nor understanding. As time progressed Nicoll's Being developed to a level at which he was not only able to communicate with Ouspensky's inner mind but could help him in his task. However, by the inexorable law of esoteric schools, when this point is reached the pupil has to be told to leave, and attempt to teach independently.

This is by no means easy for it is truly an adventure into the unknown. A mere recital of the basic principles, however faithfully remembered, is of no avail. They must have been brought into one's Being by persistent practical application so that there can develop an individual understanding which can be communicated to others. Nor is it sufficient merely to copy the methods of one's teacher. There must be a combination of integrity and initiative. As is said in the Bhagavad Gita (3rd Adhyaya v. 35) 'Better one's own way of life – *dharma* – even if it lacks merit, than that of another, even if well performed. The way of another is fraught with danger; salvation comes only by following one's own way.'

Thus it was that in September 1931, ten years after his first meeting with Ouspensky, Nicoll was to his surprise authorised to teach the Work for himself. 'Better go away', said Ouspensky reluctantly, adding after a long pause, 'Go away – and teach the System.' This necessitated complete independence from the main group, and the assembly of a nucleus of his own. It was a right decision because this new group flourished, partly in London and partly at a farm near Rayne in Essex.

When war came in 1939 Dr. Nicoll moved to Birdlip in Gloucestershire, from which after a short while he began to issue weekly papers which were read and discussed at a number of sub-groups in various parts of London and the Home Counties. These activities are described in detail, including the meetings with Gurdjieff and Ouspensky, in Beryl Pogson's biography mentioned earlier.[7]

After the war the group, now over 200 strong, moved to Great Amwell House in Hertfordshire where full-scale school activities were possible, and in 1949 the weekly papers which had been written since May 1941 were collected and published, at first privately, but later publicly, as *Psychological Commentaries on the Teaching of G. I. Gurdjieff and P. D. Ouspensky* – familiarly and now widely known as The Commentaries. They have proved invaluable to many people throughout the world, especially because of their personal quality which gives the reader the feeling that he is being spoken to individually.

Nicoll, with his deep affection for Ouspensky, had kept in touch with him through the years, particularly after his return from America shortly before his death in 1949. He continued to teach his group until his own death in 1953, having meanwhile completed three further books. One, *Living Time*, which has become a classic, was the outcome of ten years work and incorporated some of Ouspensky's thinking, while the other two, *The New Man* and *The Mark*, were concerned with new and stimulating interpretations of the Christian gospels. His group continued in existence for a time but later split into smaller units, directed by some of his principal pupils, which are still flourishing today.

14

Lyne Place

The year 1935 ushered in a further period of change. The group had increased in number and Ouspensky felt the need to establish a larger and more commodious headquarters. There was once again this sense of urgency arising from his intuitive memory which foresaw that Europe was moving inexorably towards an even more disastrous war. The masses were hypnotised by their leaders in the belief that the threat would not actually materialise so that there was no real cause for alarm.

Ouspensky remembered only too well the similar false sense of security which had prevailed prior to the 1914 war, and said that the same thing was happening again. He reminded his group of the legend of the magician who owned a large flock of sheep. These lived quite happily until they began to notice that from time to time some of them would disappear and were rumoured to have been killed and eaten. Not surprisingly they started to escape in increasing numbers so that the magician had to employ shepherds and dogs to prevent them from straying.

This soon became expensive, until he devised a very simple solution. He put them under a spell which caused them to believe that they were not sheep but lions, or eagles, or even men, in full command of their own destiny, and if there were occasional disappearances it would not happen to them – at any rate not just yet. After this there was no more trouble. The sheep once again lived in the happy belief that all was for the best.

Ouspensky considered that humanity at that time was in a similar situation and with the imminence of world conflict it seemed imperative to increase the facilities for the development of consciousness. Arrangements were made to acquire a large house called Lyne Place near Sevenoaks, some twenty miles from London. It was a beautiful estate in a lightly wooded location with a small lake adjacent to the house. It also included a flourishing farm which not only provided opportunities for work but supplied useful produce for the occupants. It was in some ways reminiscent of the Prieuré and began to accommodate an increasing number of residents.

Here it seemed that opportunities might exist for the creation of an ark in which, as in Noah's Ark of biblical legend, essential truths might be preserved against the deluge of false values. As was said earlier, Ouspensky was convinced of the existence of what he called the Great Source, the fountainhead of esoteric wisdom, but its influences could not be received, still less understood, until man's mind had been reawakened.

This involves the *metanoia* or expansion of the mind of which Christ constantly spoke, and this requires a twofold endeavour. The first part is concerned with the acquisition of (real) knowledge but this has then to be applied practically in order to produce a corresponding development of Being. The Being of anything is usually defined as its essential nature but it can be interpreted in the much wider sense of its place and purpose in the Universe. In these terms it is clear that there are many different levels of Being. Man asleep, performing his daily tasks mechanically with no self-awareness, is merely a part of life on Earth and only serves the requirements of that level. If he can carry out his various activities consciously the quality of his experiences is changed and they become of use to a higher level; in which case his level of Being is raised.

This was the aspect of the work at Lyne Place with which Madame Ouspensky was principally concerned. The Being of humanity at large is characterised by multiplicity. In the customary state of sleep man's behaviour is determined by the response of one or other of a large number of I's which have been established by experience and are brought into play by the random impact of events. If there is to be any development of consciousness these many I's have to be recognised as actually existing in oneself, and not as mere academic concepts.

To this end Madame, as she was generally referred to with a mixture of affection and awe, would administer psychological shocks to individual members at appropriate times. These were sometimes gentle, at others rough and hurtful to one's pride, but one came to realise that they were all designed to disturb the complacent belief in one's self-importance. It was a salutary and practical experience if one could tolerate it and since Ouspensky had become increasingly withdrawn many people came to regard Madame as the real leader of the group.

Robert de Ropp, who spent some time at Lyne Place, records some of his experiences in his book *Warrior's Way*.[5] He says that because Madame understood and worked on the emotional mind she was able in a space of half an hour to conduct a pupil through the whole gamut of emotions from despair to exaltation. His own feelings ranged from overwhelming dislike to something approaching adoration and he says that she gave him the most direct experience of awakening of any of his teachers.

She also knew the altered state of consciousness which can be produced by very hard physical work and on one occasion when he had spent an exhausting afternoon in the fields she said, 'See Mr. de Ropp. Usually he full of self-importance, like bishop. Now he too tired to be self-important. He man after hard day's work, like peasant.' And at that moment he was glad to be a peasant.

Later she suddenly said, 'What your chief animal?' to which he replied, 'I am not sure. Probably peacock.' She nodded. 'Yes peacock – showing off. Today you separate from peacock. You in good state. Other times you not see; you *are* peacock.'

These brief extracts illustrate very well how she was able to strip off the False Personality, and in such a way that the pupil could afterwards do it for himself, if he remembered. But there were some who could not laugh at themselves, people well-known in public life, who could not tolerate the affronts to their self-esteem and left the group, often with disparaging comments.

The Fourth Way is not for everybody. It is only for those who are prepared to pay – not in worldly goods but in the surrender of the False Personality. This requires honesty and persistence and many people find the price too high and give up the effort, preferring the comfort of their established habits. Madame made it clear that the way was hard and could not be achieved by sitting around meditating which she said was a useless practice. 'You meditate', she said, 'stare at wall. Soon you see things – angels, devils, anything. All imagination. Must work.'

After a time one begins to see that work on Being is an impersonal exercise. As the mind becomes freed from the incessant demands of the False Personality a new perspective begins to emerge. One sees the events of life as part of a cosmic plan in which one is glad to be participating.

* * *

Ouspensky himself was becoming increasingly aloof. He had lost the companionship of Maurice Nicoll, whom he had sent away to form his own group, so that he had to make his way alone. Actually he was embarking on the last lap of his journey. This may seem surprising since he was only 56 and was to live for a further 13 years. The real journey, however, is not measured in years but in terms of the expenditure of energy of which successive quanta occupy progressively longer periods of clock time. This idea was developed by Rodney Collin, a pupil of Ouspensky's, who postulated that the pattern of the life was logarithmic, involving three periods of equal energy content but of successively ten times the duration. The life must be assumed to start with conception so that the first phase is the period of gestation lasting 9 months. Next is the childhood phase during which the personality is formed, which lasts for 90 months, or $7\frac{1}{2}$ years. Finally there is the period of maturity lasting 75 years. Through each of these periods the progress is not uniform but is also logarithmic so that in the mature phase the last 20 years is equivalent to only two years experience in the first flush of youth.

The incidence and duration of this last phase is not rigid but varies with the individual. However it is a period of great significance if properly understood. It is, in fact, the last stage in an ascending octave which culminates in the change of state from the physical to the spiritual level. Hence if the life is to be a conscious exercise the activities during this final stage should not be a mere repetition of the earlier experiences but should involve a conscious integration of the whole of the pattern of the life. This would create an awareness in the whole time-body, an objective assessment of a still-existing pattern in the real world, together with all the connections and relationships with the people and situations which have been encountered during the journey through the passing time of the senses. If this can be achieved it creates a certain measure of conscious energy so that when the body ultimately dies the soul has an adequate supply of food with which to continue its adventure. This is one of the aspects of the theory of recurrence, which says that without this supply of spiritual material the life has to be repeated.

In retrospect, it seems that the tragedy of Ouspensky's life lay in his inability to recognise this opportunity. In life one's choice of action is almost completely restricted. All the reactions are determined by the responses to the established programmes of education and experience, sometimes subject to an overriding direction from a higher authority, as when some particular role has to be played. But at certain places there is a free choice. One is given a limited number of opportunities, particularly in the concluding phase.

Ouspensky did not see that his role had already been fulfilled with the establishment of Lyne Place and the completion of *In Search of the Miraculous*, which has provided posterity with a remarkably lucid and authoritative presentation of the teaching.

This could have released him for the development of the new and more emotional understanding of which there were traces in his earlier books, written from his own person before he met Gurdjieff. Yet he had written nothing of his own in these later years, nor even ventured into such realms, except perhaps in his conversations with Maurice and Catherine Nicoll. In his public utterances and written records he was careful to preserve the details of the teaching as he had received it. Yet one cannot but regret that he did not augment this with a more individual exposition, allowing freer rein to the uninhibited genius of his St. Petersburg days.

His main concern, however, prompted by the sense of urgency, was the presentation of the teaching to an ever-widening audience. He continued to give talks to his group at Warwick Gardens, which were attended by sixty to seventy people. The lectures were usually read by one of the senior pupils, often J. G. Bennett, followed by questions which Ouspensky would then answer.

These London meetings, however, were increasingly intellectual and Stanley Nott, who was to become an intimate associate of his declining years, said that whereas in the early days of the independence from Gurdjieff his lectures were full of inspiration, these later meetings were more and more unsatisfying. The talk was too theoretical and often left a feeling of emptiness, of emotional hunger.

The fact was that Ouspensky had lost his way and was living on stale manna. Robert de Ropp records that after supper on his return from a London meeting Ouspensky would often talk with some of the residents far into the night; but instead of the hoped-for pearls of wisdom the conversation was mainly reminiscences of his early days in Moscow and St. Petersburg. He was still chained to the Russia of his youth.

Meanwhile, driven by his obsession with the need for increased publicity for the teaching, he began to contemplate the formation of what he called the Historico-Psychological Society which could attract large numbers of people and through which it might be possible to organise expeditions to the East in search of the truths with which he felt that Gurdjieff had made only a partial contact.

In a tentative prospectus he declared its aims to be:

1. The study of man's true evolution, and the necessity for new systems of thought.
2. The study of esoteric schools in different historical periods and countries and their influences on the development of humanity.
3. The practical attainment of conscious living through the techniques of *psycho-transformism*.

Madame would have nothing to do with these grandiose ideas which she treated with open ridicule, much to Ouspensky's discomfiture. Nevertheless, his natural obstinacy impelled him to continue to make plans for the achievement of the idea, including a search for suitable premises in London which he was able to find some years later.

In the interim he occupied himself with writing a series of essays on Work topics such as memory, self-remembering, negative emotions and the development of will, together with some ideas on his favourite theme of recurrence. It was useful material which he used from time to time for his lectures. Much later it was collated by Merrily E. Taylor of Yale University and issued under the title of *Conscience* in 1978.

All this work was interrupted however by the sudden illness of Madame, who was no longer able to direct the operations at Lyne Place. Ouspensky himself had to take over the direction, assisted by some of the senior residents, and although in due time Madame recovered the wind of change was already freshening and a new chapter was about to commence.

15

America

In 1938 the threat of war, which Ouspensky had foreseen for some time, prompted him to increase his campaign. Events were moving rapidly towards a state of chaos in which it was essential to preserve the idea of higher levels of consciousness. After Neville Chamberlain's meeting with Hitler in October, which produced a temporary respite, he spoke of the responsibility which rested on those who had even a partial understanding of the need to awaken. If this understanding is not nurtured one will lose everything, certainly the possibility of acquiring anything more. 'Try to think', he said, 'that I may have to go away, or that the Work, as it is now, may disappear. Do not take it for granted as a permanent institution.'

He set up a new London establishment at Colet Gardens, Barons Court, W.14, which had a large lecture hall. This gave him the opportunity to put into practice the concept of the Historico-Psychological Society and as a first move he embarked on a series of public lectures which attracted audiences of 500 to 1000 people. He prepared a course of six lectures on the basic theme that while a man believes himself to be fully conscious his behaviour is actually that of a machine. This responds to impressions received by the senses in a manner which becomes entirely automatic and is not subject to any conscious control. While this idea may at first be offensive to one's vanity he goes on to show that the body which we inhabit is a truly remarkable mechanism capable of far more than its customary behaviour once its potentialities are properly understood.

These lectures were read by one of the members of his group, after which Ouspensky would answer questions from the audience. He stressed that it was necessary to attend all six lectures because it was impossible to begin to understand these new patterns of thought from only one talk, and the majority did in fact attend the full course.

Encouraged by the interest which these talks aroused he decided to print the lectures in book form, for which purpose he installed a small printing press at Colet Gardens which was operated by one of his group who had experience of the art. Evidently he had in mind that they would serve as an introduction to a continuing course of lectures, but all plans were disrupted by the outbreak of war in the autumn of 1939 and actually only about a hundred copies were completed and only a few were issued.

Because of the turmoil of war, which most people had believed would never really take place, Ouspensky's lectures did not produce the practical response he had hoped for. People were distracted by the changing conditions and instead of realising that the need for consciousness was even more urgent they decided that this was a luxury which would have to be deferred until a more peaceful time.

This, of course, was not true of the established groups which adapted themselves to the altered conditions in a fully practical manner. No-one was sure of what the future would hold, so reasonable precautions were taken. Lyne Place was equipped with stores and facilities to house members of the group if an evacuation of London became necessary, the object being to establish a haven not for personal survival so much as the preservation of the teaching.

By 1940, however, it was clear that war-time restrictions would make any large-scale continuation of the Work in England impossible. There was civilian as well as military conscription, rationing of food and services, and evening conditions were hampered by the black-out, and later by bombing. After the fall of France, Ouspensky knew that the war would last several years and so he decided to leave for America, where conditions appeared more favourable to the continuation of the campaign. Madame left early in 1941, followed a few months later by Ouspensky himself.

It was a welcome relief for Madame after her illness. She went to stay with some of her American pupils in Rumson, New Jersey, where she was visited by Stanley Nott who was in New York at the time.[6] He notes that she looked well and had evidently benefited from the change. Moreover, away from Lyne Place she no longer had need to adopt her protective facade, and displayed her natural warmth coupled with the understanding which gave her such inner strength. They spoke a great deal about Gurdjieff and the reception of his ideas in America.

Later they were joined by Ouspensky who invited Nott to lunch at the New York hotel where he was staying with two of his pupils from England. He spoke of the possibility of starting groups in America and Nott told him that though Orage had died some years earlier, his group was still operating and a meeting was arranged in Muriel Draper's house on Madison Avenue. It was not successful. The group found Ouspensky too coldly intellectual and lacking the emotional authority which they had come to expect from Gurdjieff and Orage himself.

Nott felt that, perhaps from an unusual nervousness, Ouspensky had not done himself justice and he assembled a small group, including some of Orage's pupils, with whom regular meetings could be arranged. With characteristic independence he refused to accept any fees for these meetings but said that any money which was collected should be sent to Gurdjieff in Paris. The group quickly grew, reinforced by a number of former pupils from England, but although the meetings stimulated new methods of thinking they were still typically intellectual.

America

Once again Madame attempted to supply the emotional content. A large house and estate called Franklin Farms in Mendham, New Jersey, had been put at Ouspensky's disposal and here Madame was able to organise practical work as she had done at Lyne Place in England, assisted in this case by her grandson, Lonia. As before, the emphasis was on the development of Being, which is an essential part of the teaching since knowledge alone is insufficient. Gurdjieff used to say that understanding is the product of knowledge and Being, and Madame from her days at the Prieuré was well aware of this requirement.

Yet there was always a limitation arising from the persistent refusal to allow any discussion of Gurdjieff. Stanley Nott, who visited Madame at Mendham, remonstrated with her at this attitude which he felt was senseless. The object of the group was the practice of Gurdjieff's system of ideas, which Ouspensky had always acknowledged and tried most loyally to interpret, and to refuse to allow Gurdjieff to be mentioned was like trying to teach Christianity while forbidding any reference to Jesus.

Madame became very angry, and when later she discovered that he had spoken about Gurdjieff to two members of the group, not actually resident at Mendham but still associated with it, she insisted that he should leave at once. It was evident that despite their former pleasant association she also had succumbed to the inflexible Russian attitude of her husband. Actually in this intolerant attitude Madame did not display her usual understanding. The ban on reference to Gurdjieff had been imposed by Ouspensky at the time when he began to operate independently. It was necessary to avoid the confusion which might arise from a divided allegiance. When a pupil is authorised to form his own group he has to avoid mere repetition of his teacher's method and has to devise his own tactics based on his individual and developing understanding; this necessarily requires the acceptance of his sole and unquestioned authority. But this acceptance must arise from understanding and not from blind obedience which can only degenerate into dogma, as has so often happened in orthodox religions.

* * *

Ouspensky meanwhile was concentrating his efforts on his endeavours to make the system more widely known. He only visited Mendham occasionally, spending most of his time in New York. He was concerned with the growing violence of the war in Europe and was particularly distressed when Germany attacked Russia in 1941, which he had not expected to happen and which he said he did not remember from his previous recurrence.

He felt it even more imperative to awaken people's minds and in addition to the weekly meetings of his group he began to arrange public lectures on the subject of increased consciousness. He decided to revive the six introductory lectures which he had published in England shortly before he left. A few copies had been issued then and a small number remained. He condensed the original six lectures into five chapters and wrote a general introduction illustrating the entirely mechanical nature of man's ordinary consciousness and the steps which can be taken to develop a real consciousness. However, about this time America herself became involved in the war following the attack on Pearl Harbour, and public attention became directed to more immediate and supposedly more important matters, as had been the case in England, so that the activities in New York had to be curtailed and the projected book had to be set aside. However, it did see the light of day some years later when Madame Ouspensky arranged for it to be published posthumously in 1950 under the title of *The Psychology of Man's Possible Evolution*.

At this time (1943) Ouspensky was beginning to decline. He was then 65 and no longer had the vigour of his earlier days, in addition to which he was beginning to suffer from the onset of the debilitating illness which ultimately caused his death a few years later. He was disappointed by his failure to achieve greater recognition of Gurdjieff's philosophy to which he had devoted so many years. He still had not recognised that his work had been done and that he should have been taking the opportunity to be more concerned with his own inner development even at this eleventh hour. In his early days in London he was asked by Bennett whether the practice of the ideas of this system would in time lead to an increase of consciousness. 'It may be,' said Ouspensky, 'One cannot be sure. I am not sure of anything; but I believe that this System provides the only basis of approach which is available to us at the present time.' He considered that orthodox religion had degenerated into dogma and was no longer a conscious force. This, of course, was the voice of his intellect which was always seeking a clearly defined path.

This was Damien talking, the logical faculty which caused him so much trouble. Yet one feels that when he listened to his heart rather than his head he *was* sure, because the emotional mind is in contact with the eternal truths which are not expressible in words. As Christ said, the Kingdom of Heaven is within one and is always accessible if one can learn to listen to its voice.

During these last few years, however, this seems to have been increasingly difficult for Ouspensky, who was becoming ever more lonely. He had no-one to whom he could turn. Stanley Nott had returned to England and he received no help from Madame, who was slowly becoming crippled with multiple sclerosis. So he had to contend with his own increasing infirmity alone and began to drink heavily, which inevitably aggravated the kidney complaint which was sapping his strength. Yet he says that this was the only thing he could do to relieve his boredom. He was clearly disappointed with the apparent failure of his lifelong crusade and could only play out the rest of his life as best he could.

We can only surmise the intensity of the inner struggle to remember himself which must have been involved during this very trying period. That this effort was made there can be no doubt, despite the appearance of despair. When the body is ailing it appropriates for its own needs most of the available energy, leaving little to spare for conscious control of the little I's who are only too ready to take advantage of the situation. In retrospect, one can see that Ouspensky began to prepare himself to meet his death consciously by seeking a more propitious environment.

He had never been really happy in America in which he found the psychological atmosphere too dense. He would have liked to return to his native land, but the atmosphere there had become entirely worldly, and in any case such a journey would have been quite impracticable. Only in England did he feel that there would be a congenial climate so that he began to make preparations accordingly. Madame was neither willing nor able to accompany him, so he went ahead on his own and in 1947 set sail for England again.

16

Last Days in England

In January 1947 he was able to complete the arrangements for his return to England. He found conditions very difficult; the country was still recovering from the effects of war. There were shortages of all kinds. Rationing was still in force and the London premises at Colet Gardens were still in the hands of the Military Authorities who had requisitioned them at the outset of the war.

He pulled together about a dozen members of his former group and learned what they had been doing during the war. Several of them had formed their own sub-groups and had continued to hold meetings as and when circumstances permitted in order to preserve some continuity of endeavour. Now that the war was over and Ouspensky had been able to return to England they hoped that it would be possible to resume the activities at Lyne Place and once more organise school work.

Ouspensky roughly shattered this complacent assumption by telling them that he was abandoning his role as a teacher and that they would have to make their own arrangements for the continuation of the teaching. This was received with some consternation and indeed was not fully understood by some of them, one of whom reported that Ouspensky had said that he was abandoning the System. This, of course, was a misrepresentation of a situation which they should have foreseen for themselves. The essence of the Gurdjieff philosophy, which has been called esoteric Christianity, lies in the emotional perception of truths and relationships of a higher order than those of life. To understand this, however, it is necessary to cultivate new patterns of thought and behaviour, for which purpose specific instructions have been formulated. Any such system, however, is no more than an instrument of consciousness and it has continually to be reapplied to meet changing conditions. Ouspensky thus had to tell his pupils to go out and transmit the ideas for themselves, using such understanding as they had been able to acquire. Only by making this individual excursion into unknown territory can any help be received from higher levels.

At the same time he continued to try to introduce the ideas to new people while he was still able to do so. He acquired a hall capable of seating several hundred people and began to give lectures to the public on similar lines to those which he had adopted when he had first come to London, because the climate was again suitable. The war-weary public was seeking new and more meaningful values and was ready to listen to new ideas. As before, his principal theme was that although man believes himself to be fully conscious his actual behaviour is that of a machine which responds automatically to the well-worn programmes of habit, and that he has no real individuality unless and until he can become more aware of the situation in which he finds himself and begins to understand something of the true purpose of his existence.

These lectures, however, severely taxed his failing strength and left him inwardly depleted. In preparation for his death which he now knew to be imminent he endeavoured to invigorate his time-body by reviving the memory of incidents and places which had been of more conscious significance in his experience. Many of these, of course, could only be recollected mentally. Ordinary memory is not only very fallible, but it is entirely subjective, interpreting the events in the most favourable light, and it is almost always contaminated by nostalgia. However, there is also interior memory, which is a conscious revisiting of the event or situation in one's time-body. In some cases the memory can be refreshed by actually returning to places having these significant associations. He therefore arranged to be driven around the country to those places which were still accessible physically, such as his old flat in Gwendwr Road and the house at Gadsden, and Alley Cottage in Sussex where he had spent so many pleasant weekends with Catherine and Maurice Nicoll.

His recollections were not always happy, because he was at this time a very lonely old man and sought solace in increasing quantities of his favourite Montrachet. He was particularly distressed by the complete loss of contact with Gurdjieff and one evening said tearfully to his faithful friend, Stanley Nott, 'Why does he not talk to me? Does he not know that I love him?' Are we to disparage him, as some have done, for an occasional cry of despair in his infirmity?

Again, in retrospect one can understand something of his attempts to enliven his time-body. The idea of recurrence had interested him most of his life and he wrote about it in detail in some of his earlier books. The discussions however were intellectual, concerned with the possible mechanism of this strange idea, and it was not until much later that he began to feel the actual existence of the time-body as a kind of track in a higher dimensional world, parts of which were then actualised in succession by the passage of time. Once this concept is visualised the whole meaning and purpose of existence takes on a different aspect. One can see that the pattern of the life has already been created by the soul as a framework of opportunities which can then be utilised in the fulfilment of a spiritual purpose. Full use of these opportunities cannot be made in a single life but if the role has been played with some degree of consciousness a kind of spiritual memory begins to form. The life can then be repeated with a more conscious understanding until, in time, the possibilities are fully utilised and the soul is released.

This is an idea requiring emotional perception which can

only be developed by individual effort. One can surmise that Ouspensky explored this territory with his customary insight but unfortunately refused to commit himself, possibly because it was not regarded as part of the System. He rarely gave expression to his personal aspirations, which would have transformed the whole quality of his writing, but this was the role he had to play and it included the unhappiness of his later years. It is in the playing of the role that life is fulfilled, not in the role itself.

* * *

His health began to deteriorate rapidly, perhaps because he felt that he had done all that was required of him so that there was no longer any need to inhabit his ailing and uncomfortable body. It was evident that his death would not be long delayed, but when it finally happened on October 2nd, 1947, it had a strangely triumphant quality. The day before, he appeared unexpectedly, fully dressed, and summoned the household for a final briefing. He spoke to them in terms of great affection. He emphasised that each of them had to make a fresh start, reconstructing from the very beginning all that they had learned and then venturing boldly into the unknown territory wherein they would find help. The atmosphere was alive with conscious influences which were communicated wordlessly to the assembled company in such a way that each perceived individually the way ahead.

Unseen presences were all around in what appeared to be the prelude to a conscious and joyous transition from the physical to the spiritual state. Ouspensky had at last cast off the shackles of his role. He left the room and retired to bed, where he died peacefully the following day.

* * *

Maurice Nicoll had kept in touch with Ouspensky after his

return from America and actually sent him two paintings of Sidlesham to remind him of their happy days together at Alley Cottage. When he received news of Ouspensky's death he spoke to his group privately about their many experiences together, not in any atmosphere of lamentation but rather as an occasion of joyful remembrance. He reminded them of Gurdjieff's condemnation of the many conventional condolences which had poured in on the death of Orage in America. These he said were utterly useless and indeed did great harm to the person who had just died. In ancient times in fact it was considered criminal.

Both Maurice and Catherine Nicoll had been very fond of Ouspensky and he spoke of the warmth and humour which Ouspensky had displayed in his less formal moments. He also mentioned a dream which he had had during the early days of their association in which Ouspensky had appeared as a bird whose feathers were constantly being ruffled by gusts of wind but who remained unmoved, quite impervious to these minor irritations. This was Ouspensky's great strength though in some respects his greatest weakness.

After his death Madame took charge of his affairs. Lyne Place was sold and she returned to America with all his records and documents, and with the assistance of her group she began to arrange for the publication of the works which he had written during his life. The first of these was the now widely acclaimed treatise on the teaching of Gurdjieff which was issued under the title *In Search of the Miraculous*. This appeared simultaneously with Gurdjieff's own book *All and Everything* in 1949.

Copious records existed of his many meetings and the questions and answers given to his groups. These were carefully collated by the group in America in order to present a coherent exposition of the ideas which was then published under the title *The Fourth Way* in 1952.

Madame herself died in 1963, when all Ouspensky's records were bequeathed to the Library of the University of Yale in New Haven, Connecticut, U.S.A., where they are still preserved.

17

Ouspensky Fourth Dimension

As was said earlier, in his younger days Ouspensky was often jocularly referred to by his journalistic cronies as 'Ouspensky Fourth Dimension'. This was because of his known interest in the matter which was indeed the subject of his first book, and he would often sit up far into the night discussing this and other mysteries with them. However, this is a phrase which is of far deeper significance than a light-hearted nickname, because if we are to understand this unsung genius we must look behind the appearances of the familiar world.

In his early days, the fourth dimension was regarded as something mysterious and abstract, and even today many people consider it so. Actually, Ouspensky himself was at pains to demolish this spurious mystique by showing that the fourth dimension is an entirely practical concept which is unfamiliar simply because in the ordinary way we take it for granted. The shape and position of any object in the familiar world is defined in terms of the three dimensions of space, namely length, depth and height. But everything is constantly changing, sometimes quickly, sometimes almost imperceptibly slowly and these changes are the result of movement along a fourth dimension, the dimension of time. We measure this movement in terms of seconds, hours, days or years according to circumstances.

However, just because an object has changed its condition does not mean that it has ceased to exist. Our senses only perceive the state of an object at the present moment. By the use of memory we can recall its position at some earlier time and by inference we can estimate what the situation will be at some future time. This is all that is required for the purposes of day-to-day existence, which is conducted by an automatic and virtually unconscious blend of perception and reasoning. Yet it is clear that in reality the whole situation is continually existing and that it is only the senses which create the illusion of the present moment. Every object in fact has its own time-body which has an actual and relatively permanent existence in the real world.

We really live in this four-dimensional world though our ordinary senses do not perceive it. However, we do have a range of little-used additional senses we call intuition which can assess the real situation and by using this it is possible to lead a conscious existence. In quite practical terms this means that every man and women has his or her own time-body which interacts with the time-bodies of every other person or situation with which they come in contact during their transit through life. This is an idea of great depth for it means that we do not exist in isolation. As John Donne said in the familiar words, 'No man is an Island'.

It is in these terms that one must try to understand Ouspensky. His life must be seen not as a succession of events in passing time, a succession of events and situations on which we, in our self-centred blindness, are only too ready to sit in judgment. Actually, the time-body of any individual is not an accidental entity. It is a pattern in the real world which is brought into being in succession just like the successive frames of a cinematograph film. This was the analogy used by Ouspensky himself in his story of *The Strange Life of Ivan Osokin*. However, the scenes in a cinema film are created by the producer. In the same way the pattern of life in the real world must have been created by a superior intelligence and according to many ancient legends the soul is allotted a specific life which it has to undergo during its sojourn on earth. The pattern of the life depends upon the stature of the soul in question. It may be a purely perfunctory pattern designed to serve the purposes of humanity at large. However, if the soul has already acquired certain understanding it is allowed a certain choice, a choice which will be determined not by considerations of personal comfort or success but by the opportunities which it may provide for further development. In addition, as Ouspensky points out in *A New Model of the Universe*, there are some roles which are prescribed for cosmic purposes such as kings and emperors, politicians, leaders of industry, explorers and innovators, scientists and so forth, all of which have to be played without variation for the purposes of history. These roles are allotted to already well-developed souls who can play them consciously, not attempting to vary the performance but extracting from it spiritual nourishment. The events of life involve the expenditure of energy which is utilised in the maintenance of the physical world. However, if they can be experienced consciously the quality of the energy is changed and it can be used for individual benefit.

Superficially one may not see how public, and possibly evil, characters can be playing a conscious role though it is more understandable in the case of spiritual leaders. There can be no doubt that both Ouspensky and his wife were playing conscious roles in association with Gurdjieff, Maurice Nicoll and others, all of whom were serving the requirements of the Conscious Circle of Humanity. Ouspensky's role in particular was that of formulation which his genius for lucidity of expression enabled him to fulfil with outstanding merit. It is only a partial approach because true understanding requires the use of the emotional mind which operates at the level of the higher intelligences which direct the unmanifest patterns of existence. In bygone days this was used as a matter of course, but in the process of time the intuitive faculties became atrophied and today for the majority of people contact with these higher levels can only be re-established through the intellectual faculty. Hence Ouspensky's role, of the greatest service to humanity, was the presentation of esoteric ideas in a form which would be acceptable to the materialistic mind of today. It was a role which involved considerable sacrifice for he would have been far happier developing his early intuitive genius instead of accepting the duty of promulgating the ideas which Gurdjieff had brought from the East, particularly since in the fulfilment of this role he had to suffer the calumnies of Gurdjieff himself.

It is necessary to see Ouspensky's life as part of a much greater pattern being operated at this period of time by the conscious levels of the Universe. The established habits of thought always regard progress as developing from past to future, but real progress in the Universe is not measured in terms of passing time but in the much greater period of astrological time. It is said that there are four ages in world progress, namely the golden age, the silver age, the bronze age and the iron age also called the age of Kali Yuga, the age of barbarism. It is evident that the world has been in this last age for a long time and is in fact on the point of transition into a fresh golden age where spiritual values will predominate. Astrologically we are about to enter the age of Aquarius which will be character-ised by consciousness and understanding and will be guided not by any single leader but by a large number of adepts in permanent communication with higher intelligences and each other, and one can recognise with delight the arrival of Ouspen-sky as one of the forerunners of this new age.

* * *

What do we owe to Ouspensky: and more important, what are we prepared to pay? The idea of payment is today almost

Ouspensky: The Unsung Genius

outmoded. Everything is demanded as of right with querulous complaints if the demands are not satisfied in full. Actually nothing in the Universe is free. There is an old Spanish proverb: 'Take what you want, says God, and pay for it.' As a corollary, nothing has lasting value unless it has been paid for.

Gurdjieff expressed this by saying that everything eats something lower than itself and is in turn eaten by something higher. The idea of payment is in some ways more readily understandable and has the merit of reminding us of the complacent manner in which we normally take everything for granted. Ouspensky had to make his own payment in which he only partially succeeded. The payment for his brilliant intellect had to be made by a life of dedication, often lonely, giving compassion but rarely receiving it. These situations could have been material for the creation of spiritual exaltation, but his emotional mind was insufficiently developed to allow this transformation to be fully achieved.

What payment then will *we* make for the enormous benefits which we have received from Ouspensky's painstaking work? Do we not take these luminous ideas which Gurdjieff brought from the Eastern Monastery as something to which we are entitled entirely free of charge? Does it ever occur to us to acknowledge the debt of gratitude which we owe to Ouspensky for his detailed expositions? All too often people criticise them as being too formatory. Presumably they feel that if they only had the time they could do it much better.

The real value of Ouspensky's writing arises in the patterns behind the words and these we can only see if we can interpret them as having been written by a man, and not a mere name – a man who was endeavouring to communicate with higher levels of consciousness and understanding of which he was intuitively aware. If we can do this with an appropriate sense of humility and gratitude we can in some measure repay our debt. In conventional terms Ouspensky died over 30 years ago and hence is now a thing of the past. The real man is still in existence in the realm of Eternity, and in his own time-scale he is at this very moment reinhabiting the life allotted to him in the endeavour to utilise to the fullest extent the opportunities which it provides. If we can give expression in our hearts to a feeling of gratitude and delight for having met him even if only through his books, we may perhaps enable him to achieve his goal more swiftly.

The most practical way of expressing our gratitude to Ouspensky is to try to develop for ourselves the understanding which he strove so patiently to communicate. As was said, the system of ideas which was introduced by Gurdjieff provides an extremely practical method of attaining a measure of real consciousness. It is not to be seen as an end in itself, but rather as a means whereby the spirit may escape from its bondage. If by its use a state of self-remembering can be attained, even if only briefly, the way is opened for a real adventure, which is not a journey in passing time with its continual expectation of result but is an excursion within the timeless realm of eternity, which contains the underlying patterns of existence.

In this state one is no longer a separate individual but is part of what Zen Buddhism calls The Totality Which is One; and the effort involved contributes to the pool of cosmic consciousness and enables us to reinforce each other and in particular our teachers in the so-called past.

Relevant Reading

After Ouspensky's death all his papers were bequeathed to the Library of the University of Yale, New Haven, Connecticut, U.S.A., and a fund was set up for the collation and preservation of these records. As part of this activity a commemorative brochure was published in 1978, the centenary of his birth, entitled *Remembering Pyotr Demianovich Ouspensky*, which contains brief biographical notes together with selected recollections of those who knew him.

Reference to the Ouspenskys can also be found in the following books:

1. Bennett, J. G.
   Gurdjieff. Making a New World (Turnstone Press 1973).
2. Bennett, J. G.
   Witness (Turnstone Press, 1975).
3. Butkovsky-Hewitt, Anna
   With Gurdjieff in St. Petersburg and Paris (Routledge & Kegan Paul, 1978).
4. Collin, Rodney
   The Theory of Celestial Influence (Vincent Stuart, 1954).
5. De Ropp, Robert S.
   Warrior's Way (George Allen & Unwin, 1980).
6. Nott, C. S.
   Further Teachings of Gurdjieff (Routledge & Kegan Paul, 1969).
7. Pogson, Beryl
   Maurice Nicoll. A Portrait (Vincent Stuart, 1961).
8. Walker, Kenneth
   Venture with Ideas (Jonathan Cape, 1951).
9. Webb, James
   The Harmonious Circle (Thames & Hudson, 1968).

Some discussion of the ideas of recurrence which so greatly intrigued Ouspensky can be found in the author's own book *No Easy Immortality* (George Allen & Unwin) wherein it is shown that the survival of the spirit is not to be thought of as a future state but is an adventure in the realms of eternity.

Major Books by P. D. Ouspensky

Tertium Organum
A Key to the Enigmas of the World (Routledge & Kegan Paul).

A New Model of the Universe
Principles of the Psychological Method in its application to the problems of Science, Religion and Art (Routledge & Kegan Paul).

Letters from Russia 1919
(Routledge & Kegan Paul, 1978).

In Search of the Miraculous
Fragments of an Unknown Teaching (Routledge & Kegan Paul).

The Fourth Way
A Record of Talks and Answers to Questions based on the teaching of G. I. Gurdjieff (Routledge & Kegan Paul).

The Psychology of Man's Possible Evolution
Six introductory talks to prospective students of the Gurdjieff teaching (Hodder & Stoughton).

The Strange Life of Ivan Osokin
The semi-autobiographical novel involving the ideas of recurrence (Faber & Faber, 1947).

Talks with a Devil
Two short stories written by Ouspensky in his St. Petersburg days, with an introduction by J. G. Bennett (Turnstone Press).

The Symbolism of the Tarot Cards
Written during his early researches and later incorporated in *A New Model of the Universe* (Dover Publications, New York, 1976).

Conscience
A series of essays written in his later London period, collated and introduced by Merrily E. Taylor (Routledge & Kegan Paul, 1979).